# The Wilmot Story

## The Search for Who We Are

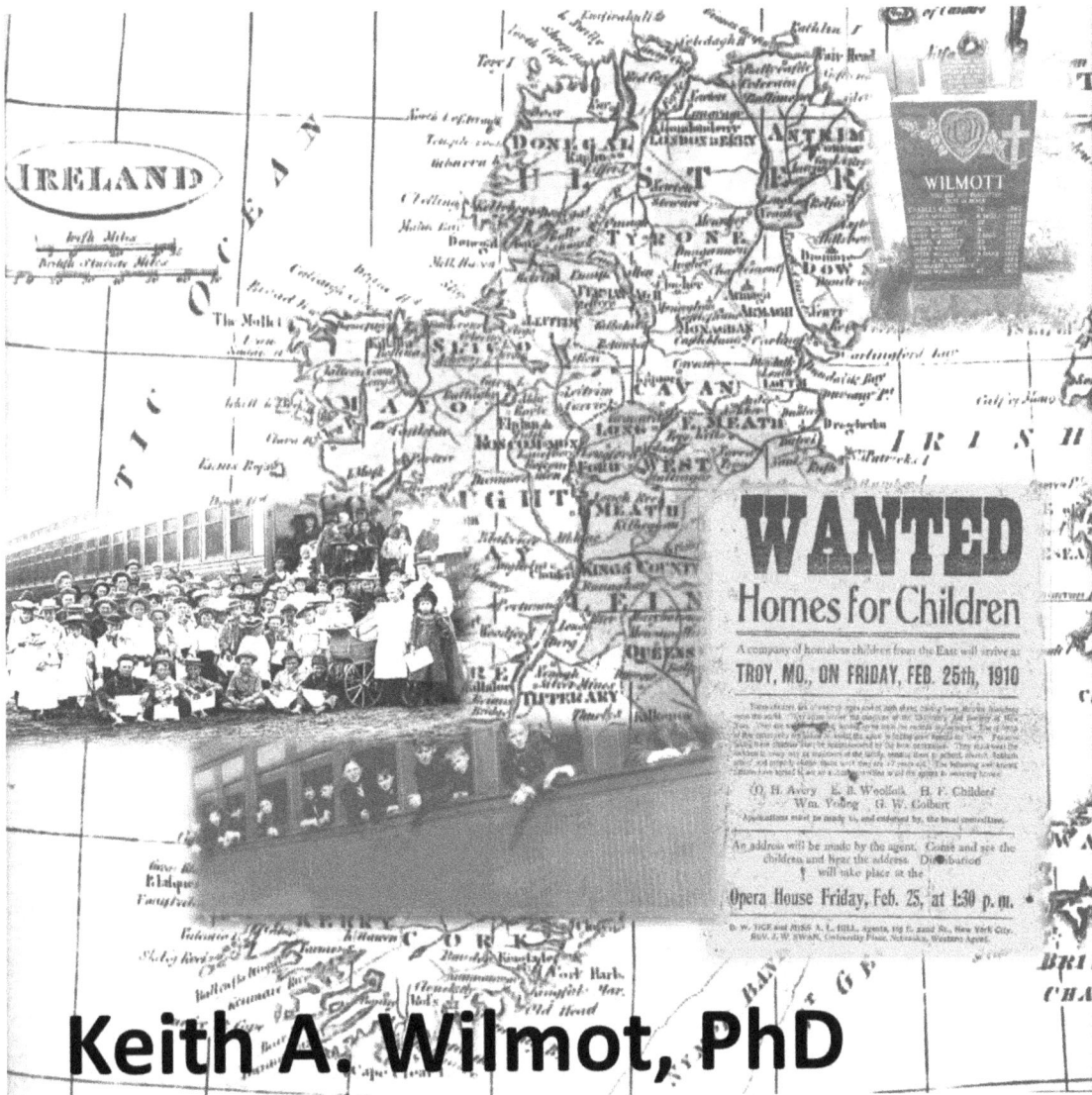

# Keith A. Wilmot, PhD

# The Wilmot Story
## The Search for Who We Are

The story of the Wilmot family begins in 1794, Cloyne, County Cork, Ireland, and follows a path of immigration in the early 19th century to Atlantic Canada and on to New York in the mid-19th century. The hardships, sickness, and poverty of early immigrants in Manhattan, New York, takes its toll on the Wilmot family with death and the subsequent family breakup. This leads to one orphaned Wilmot traveling to the Midwest on the legendary Orphan Train where he is placed in servitude until such age as he marries and begins a family in Missouri. We follow the family from Missouri to Nebraska where the trail ends for now. Thus, this is the story of the Wilmot family and one man's search for who we are.

## Keith A. Wilmot, PhD

Deep River Publishing
San Antonio, Texas

# The Wilmot Story
## The Search for Who We Are

Published by Deep River Publishing

San Antonio, Texas

ISBN: 978-0-578-74578-7

Library of Congress Control Number: 2020915513

1st Edition

Printed in the United States of America by IngramSpark

**This is a story dedicated to our Wilmot ancestors who came before us.**

*"I am bound to them,*
*though I cannot look into their eyes*
*or hear their voices*
*I honor their history.*
*I cherish their lives.*
*I will tell their story.*
*I will remember them."*

Author Unknown

# Acknowledgements

This ancestry narrative started out as many family trees in which the usual link chart is created by placing names, dates, and locations in sequence to illustrate a specific family lineage over time. However, as I ventured deeper with my readings and research it became more and more apparent that there were individual stories to be told. But this narrative would not have developed into the scale it has become without the support and suggestions of close friends and family noted below.

Over time, there has always been familial discussions and general charting of ancestors regarding our mother's side of the family, however, over that time, little was ever known regarding the paternal or Wilmot side of the family. Thus, with DNA findings and ancestry research the slow process began to uncover the Wilmot past. The catalyst which ultimately sparked my immersion into this quest was gratefully provided by my brother Bob who had written an inquisitive letter to the Children's Aid Society, New York, June 2015, in search of information concerning our great grandfather. The response from the Children's Aid Society was encouraging and essentially, the first step in laying the groundwork for our study. Robert was also instrumental in the narrative process by providing documents, photos, and overall knowledge of family history. His constructive suggestions following review of early manuscript drafts were most useful. Likewise, I would like to thank our brother Jim for contributing family photos and providing pertinent details to our family's history as well. Lastly, thank you to our sister Mary Lu who offered her valued assistance many times by just listening to bits of family history which would, at times, spark her recollection of early times in Missouri and early family life growing up in Omaha, Nebraska.

Next, I would like to thank C.W. 'Jim' James, genealogist extraordinaire, for his endless support through this whole process from start to finish. His initial background in ancestry research helped me in the early stages of my research which saved me considerable time as I began the search for our Wilmot ancestors. His genuine interest kept me motivated as I pursued the lengthy narrative process. He tirelessly read various drafts of the transcript and gave positive feedback. Most important were his 'techno' skills that took my original photos and rendered quality images for print and provided accurate formatting of the transcript itself. His creativity also shows through with the unique cover design for the book. In sum, Jim's previous experience with ancestry research and self-publishing helped immensely to pull all this together into a final copy for print.

Finally, I would like to thank the ongoing interest and support I received from close friends Tom and Jan McCrudden as the Irish nexus developed, especially the link to Manhattan, Tom's old stomping grounds. In turn, thanks to fellow co-worker, friend, and subject-matter expert,

Nathan Teigland, who assisted with the early stage of my ancestral research by substantiating our family connection to New York. His reminder to me early on that genealogy was very much like intelligence research; however, intelligence research is work whereas genealogy is considerably more fun. Also noteworthy was the interest provided by my son Jason who always seemed intrigued with my findings. Lastly, a huge hug and thank you to my wife Kelly for being a super-hero having offered daily support and the patience and wherewithal to listen to my self-discussions as to who, what, when, and where.

# Table of Contents

# The Wilmot Story

## A Paternal Trace

**Patrick** or Pat **Wilmot(t)** (Abt.) 1780 - (Abt.) 1838
3rd great-grandfather
**Anne Nason** (Abt.) 1778 - (Abt.) 1871
3rd great-grandmother
(Patrick 1801-unk), **Michael** 1803-1867, (Anne 1806-unk)
I
**Michael Wilmot(t)** 1803-1867
Son of Patrick or Pat Wilmot(t)
2nd great-grandfather
**Mary Collan Wilmot(t)** 1805-1880
2nd great-grandmother
(**James** 1831-1874, William 1833-1857, Ellen 1837-unk, Alice K. 1838-1928,
Mary Anne 1841-unk, Peter 1844-1892, John 1847-1901)
I
**James Wilmot(t)** 1831-1874
Son of Michael Wilmot(t)
great-grandfather
**Sophia Kline/Cline Wilmot(t)** 1837-1872
great-grandmother
(Alice 1859-unk, James 1861-1862, William Henry 1863-1933, **James A.** 1868-1941)
I
**James A. Wilmot(t)** 1868-1941
Son of James Wilmot(t)
Grandfather
**Effie Alice Sartain Wilmot(t)** 1883 - (Abt.) 1908
Grandmother
(Orville Price 1902-1986, **Noble King** 1903-1984, William Howard 1906-1939)
I
**Noble King Wilmot** 1903-1984
Son of James A. Wilmot(t)
Father
**Mary Louise Crabtree Wilmot** 1904-1969
Mother
(Mary Lu 1932-, James Noble 1941-, Robert King 1944-, Keith Alan 1947-)

# Our Search for Who We Are

We begin in Ireland the birthplace of our paternal great-great grandfather, Michael Wilmot. From a genetic perspective this seems to be a good place to start since throughout his life he always claimed to be of Irish descent. It is uncertain if Michael's father, Patrick, or his mother, Anne, were born in Ireland, or whether they were among many that migrated to Ireland as many before him had. Ireland is at least a 9,000-year-old melting pot of cultures and traditions of various individuals and groups who came to Ireland and either settled, terrorized, and pillaged, or moved on over time. In the big picture of world civilization, Ireland is a relatively recent settled country having endured the effects of two Ice Ages which limited the possibility of any long-term settlement prior to the human occupation such as that discovered at Mount Sandel in County Antrim approximately 9,000 years ago.

Over time, various groups have blended into the Irish culture. Groups such as the Celts, Picts, Vikings, Saxons, and Normans all were early migrants and settlers having brought a variety of DNA from competing cultures. Some came by land from England via Europe (at the end of the last Ice Age) and other early inhabitants came by sea from Scandinavia or as far away as Iberia. For example, one of the larger groups, the Celts, originated as a composite group of central European chieftains and their clans which over time, spread out to other lands such as Spain, Asia Minor and England, eventually making their way to Ireland, and as a result, establishing themselves as early precursors of DNA in Ireland in approximately 150 BC. However, as with other migrating groups, defining who Celts are is difficult. There is no conclusive evidence that there is an underlying ancient Celtic race; however, a Celtic lineage appears to be a culture based in language, culture, and art over time. More specifically, as Bryan Sykes notes, "Overall, the genetic structure of the Isles is stubbornly Celtic, if by that we mean descent from people who were here before the Romans and who spoke a Celtic language." [1] Other groups mentioned above have a similar foundation in Ireland.

Finally, as Marie McKeown acknowledges, "What we can take from all of this is that, although the Irish today feel part of a single group united by cultural and national identity, this culture and identity is ultimately founded on waves of migration connecting the island to the wider world of European peoples and beyond."[2]

---

[1] Sykes, B. (2006). Saxons, Vikings, and Celts, the Genetic Roots of Britain and Ireland. W.W. Norton and Company, New York, NY, page 287.

[2] McKeown, M. (2018). Blood of the Irish: What DNA Tells Us About the People in Ireland. Owlcation - Genetics & Evolution. Retrieved from https://owlcation.com/stem/Irish-Blood-Genetic-Identity.

# DNA Summary

Our Wilmot ancestral research began after having received the results of my DNA sample from Ancestry.com. Ancestry's DNA findings concluded that approximately 60 percent of my sampled DNA indicate a genetic ethnicity link to Scotland, Northern Ireland and Ireland, and 40 percent of my DNA referenced a genetic relationship with Great Britain, Wales, and Northwestern Europe (as of September 2020).[3] As a result, this research will explore our genetic ancestral roots from the United States back to the British Isles. Furthermore, based on the DNA findings (only Keith has submitted his DNA), the primary focus of this narrative is the paternal lineage of our father Noble King Wilmot (Wilmott). Upcoming research and narrative of our father's maternal side regarding the surname Sartain (Sartin, Sartan) will follow in-the-near future. In turn, similar research will continue to explore our mother's related surnames, Crabtree (paternal) and Foley (maternal), a common Irish surname.[4] For now, we begin the paternal trace of the Noble King Wilmot family.

# The WILMOT SURNAME

The foundation of the Wilmot surname reflected in our Irish percentage of DNA (Ireland/Northern Ireland) is represented in part by the paternal Wilmot(t) side of our family history. At this point in time, our ancestral link to Patrick Wilmott and Ann Nason is as far back as current research has led us. Per parish records Patrick and Ann were married in Cloyne, County Cork, Ireland, in 1794. Following their marriage, Patrick and Ann had three children: Patrick baptized in 1801, Michael baptized in 1803 and Anne baptized in 1806. All three children were baptized Catholic in the Parish/District: Aghada, County Cork, Ireland. Their second son, Michael, is our great great grandfather. Michael, in time, immigrated to New Brunswick, Canada, where in the year 1830, he met and married Mary Collan, another Irish immigrant from Urney, County Tyrone, Ireland. Michael and Mary, prior to immigrating to New York, had five children. Their son James, who was born in St. John, New Brunswick, 1831, is our paternal great grandfather.

---

[3] DNA percentages are approximations that change over time as more people test. Reference groups become more defined and algorithmic methods are further adjusted for more exact estimates.

[4] Foley (surname) The name is derived from the original modern Irish Ó Foghlú and older Irish Ó Foghladha. This interesting surname is an Anglicized form of the Old Gaelic "O'Foghladha". The Gaelic prefix "O" indicates "male descendant of", plus the personal byname "Foghladha" meaning pirate or plunderer. This great sept originated in the southern Munster County of Waterford, and from there spread to Counties Cork and Kerry, where the name is particularly widespread, and ranks among the sixty most numerous surnames in Ireland. The distinguished English family of Foley, centered in Worcestershire and its surrounding counties, is believed to be of Irish origin. In his "Dictionary of English and Welsh surnames", C.W. Bardsley, states that "Foley must be looked upon as an Irish surname". Bardsley, C.W. (1901). A Dictionary of English and Welsh Surnames. Oxford University Press.

## Surnames Explained:

This stage of our ancestral research will provide a more detailed discussion of the surnames Wilmot, Nason, Collan and Mullin. Surnames, like Y-chromosomes, are passed down the paternal line. In Ireland, there have been inherited surnames for as long as anywhere in Europe. They were first adopted in approximately 950 AD, a good 200 years earlier than in England. Many Irish surnames in the beginning were of Gaelic origin often reflected by the prefix 'Mc' or 'O', meaning 'son of', as in McCrudden or O'Neil.[5] England, in contrast, took until the end of the thirteenth century for the practice of forename and surname to take hold following the Norman Conquest when the strictly enforced feudal system insisted that estates have men adopt surnames to control for inheritance of land tenancies.[6] Over time, variations of surnames have developed and with the infusion of greater interest in genealogy, the compilation of comprehensive surname dictionaries has developed. One such source is John Grenham's website, www.johngrenham.com. This site will be used for the general review of the above noted surnames in addition to complimentary remarks by Michael Collins (Mike@youririshheritage.com).

The surname Wilmot(t) is an Anglicized English surname of Germanic pre-7th century origins. The Wilmot(t) surname appears to have transformed from the Germanic first name Wilhelm to the French form – Guillaume, to the English version – Gillam, transforming to William. The Wilmot surname and its variants apparently derived from the first name 'William' which had become extremely popular at the time. Thus, it follows that variant surnames, originating from the personal name William, developed in England following the Norman Quest. One being Wilmot(t) and its variants, as a diminutive form of the original personal name 'Wilhelm', which included the diminutive suffix 'et(t)' or 'ot(t)' meaning 'little' or possibly 'son of'.[7] Since the estimated arrival of the Wilmot(t) surname in Ireland in the early 17th century, the name has not been 'hibernicised' - transformed into an Irish form.

From an Irish perspective there are numerous variants of Wilmott, but the two most notable are Wilmott and Wilmot. According to one surname dictionary, the Wilmott surname was quite numerous and scattered in Ulster and Limerick. The name has been associated with Kerry since 1614.[8] Mike Collins noted further that, "Wilmot is a name of English origin that came to north Kerry/West Limerick in the early 1600s. The area around Cloyne and Aghada was a big garden market for the south of the island and a lot of people worked on the food farms there. I suspect that your Wilmot(t) came into the area for work - and met someone with the Nason surname (which

---

[5] Sykes, page 161.
[6] Sykes, page 272.
[7] Verstappen, P. (2018) Forebears - Wilmot Surname Meaning. Retrieved from https://forebears.io/surnames/wilmot#meaning.
[8] MacLysaght, E. (1985). Surnames of Ireland. Irish Academic Press. Kildare, Ireland. Retrieved from www.johngrenham.com.

also came from England in the 1600s) and is quite numerous and localized there".[9] The search for surnames on John Grenham's website for Irish births between 1864 and 1913 per Griffith's list of households indicates a total of 318 individuals with variants for the Wilmot/Wilmott surname (including Willmot, Willmott, Wilmet, Wilmoth, Willmoth, and Welmuth). Total recorded Roman Catholic baptisms in Ireland for the variants of the Wilmot surname is 158.[10] In contrast, the surname Nason during the same time period for the Griffith's Valuation of households only records 35 households, 28 of which were in Cork. Total recorded Roman Catholic baptisms for the Nason surname in Ireland is 101. MacLysaght's surname dictionary notes that the surname Nason was fairly rare in Ireland and found mainly in Cork having come to Ireland from England in the 17th century.[11] Collectively, this information lays the foundation for the surnames of Patrick Wilmott (3rd great grandfather) and Ann Nason (3rd great grandmother) who married in 1794, Cloyne, County Cork, Ireland.

Collan and Mullin surnames evolve from Michael Wilmott's marriage to Mary Collan (great great grandmother) in 1830, St. John, New Brunswick, Canada. Michael (great great grandfather) son of Patrick and Ann carried the surname Wilmott which has already been discussed. Mary Collan's parents, according to the marriage certificate, were John Collan (3rd great grandfather) and Eleanor Mullin (3rd great grandmother). Thus, the discussion of the surnames Collan and Mullin.

The surname Collan has many Irish variants. The search on John Grenham's website for Irish births between 1864 and 1913 per Griffith's Valuation list of households indicate a total of 168 head of households for Collan and variants which included: Collen, Collin, McCollin, McCollen, McCollan, Colen, Colin, Coln, McColin. (Of these variants, Collen (55) and Collen (49) were the most numerous.)[12] Collan had 11 recorded births during this time. Additionally, Collan and its variants only accounted for 52 head of households between 1847 and 1864 in Ireland. And finally, the 1901 and 1911 censuses indicate only one Collan head of household for each census year. Thus, it is apparent that the surname Collan and its variants were not common over time in Ireland.

---

[9] Collins, M. (2019). Your Irish Heritage. Correspondence retrieved from youririshheritage.com.

[10] Griffith's Valuation - Other than a few fragments, the Irish census records from the nineteenth century did not survive, either having been pulped for paper in the First World War or lost in the Public Record Office fire of 1922. Irish genealogists must therefore rely on records that act as 'census substitutes' to find out information about families and households. Griffith's Valuation is one of the most important sources to Irish local and family historians since it is the most comprehensive household survey that survives for the mid-nineteenth century, providing an insight into households in the period between the Famine (1847) and the start of civil registration in 1864. Griffith's Valuation. (2017). Retrieved from http://www.findmypast.com.

[11] MacLysaght.

[12] John Grenham's surname dictionary notes that the surname Collen was 'fairly rare' and a variant of Cullen in Ulster. https://www.johngrenham.com.

In contrast, the surname Mullin exists with a number of variants which are quite numerous in all areas of Ireland with wide distribution. Some of the most common surnames in addition to Mullin include the following: Mullins, Mullen, Mullan, Mullane, McMullin, McMullen, McMullan. This group of surnames represent 4,046 registered Irish head of households between 1847 and 1864. In 1901 and 1911, Ireland censuses show a total of 225 and 198 head of households respectively for the sole Mullin clan. Collectively, for all variants, there were 21,917 births between 1864 and 1913. Mullin and variants therefore appear to reflect a resilient family line during the mid-19th and early 20th centuries. Thus, in a historic context, both the Collan and Mullin surnames with their varied underpinnings do show an additional Irish nexus to *The Wilmot Story*.

# THE WILMOT STORY BEGINS

## Patrick Wilmot (3rd Great Grandfather)

The Wilmot story begins in Ireland in the late 18th century.

      Patrick (Pat) Wilmoth (Welworth) and Anne Nason were married October 24, 1794, in the Diocese of Cloyne, Cloyne Parish/District (variant forms of Cloyne parish: Churchtown, Churchtown and Kilteskin, Kilteskin), County Cork, Ireland. Their religious denomination was Roman Catholic. Their parents' names were noted as FNU Wilmoth and FNU Nason. They were married by Reverend Dr. Coppinger and witnesses included James (Js) Sisk and Ann Byrne.[13] [14] (*See below*: marriage may have taken place on either 22 or 23 of October 1794).

Pat Wilmott and Anne Nason
Ireland Roman Catholic Marriages, October 22, 1774

---

[13] Church Marriage Records - July 1794 to November 1794. *Mallow Heritage Centre* (Cloyne/Microfilm 04990/01, Page 14). Retrieved from http://www.rootsireland.ie.
[14] Ireland Catholic Parish Marriage Images. Library of Ireland. Retrieved from http://search/findmypast.com.

## Church Marriage Record

| | |
|---|---|
| Date of Marriage: | 22-Oct-1794 |
| Parish / District: | CLOYNE |

County: Co. Cork

**Husband**

| | |
|---|---|
| Name: | Patrick    Wilmoth |
| Address: | Not Recorded |
| Denomination: | Roman Catholic |
| Occupation: | |
| Age: | |
| Status: | |

**Wife**

| | |
|---|---|
| Name: | Ann    Nason |
| Address: | Not Recorded |
| Denomination: | Roman Catholic |

**Husband's Father**

| | |
|---|---|
| Name: | Wilmoth |
| Address: | |
| Denomination: | |
| Occupation: | |

**Wife's Father**

| | |
|---|---|
| Name: | Nason |

**Husband's Mother**

| | |
|---|---|
| Name: | |
| Address: | |
| Denomination: | |
| Occupation: | |

**Wife's Mother**

**Witness 1**

| | |
|---|---|
| Name: | James    Sisk |
| Address: | |

**Witness 2**

| | |
|---|---|
| Name: | Ann    Byrne |

**Notes:**

CELEB: RT. REV. DR. COPPINGER. HUSBAND'S PET NAME (PAT). WIFE'S
NAME SPELT AS (ANNE). 1ST. WIT. NAME E 1/8).THIS ENTRY CAME FROM A
COPIED
REGISTER,CLOYNE MARRAIGES 1,BUT CONTAINS ALL INFORMATION FROM THE
ORIGINAL
REGISTER

Patrick Wilmoth and Ann Nason
"Church Marriage Record," October 22, 1794
*Mallow Heritage Centre* (Cork North and East)

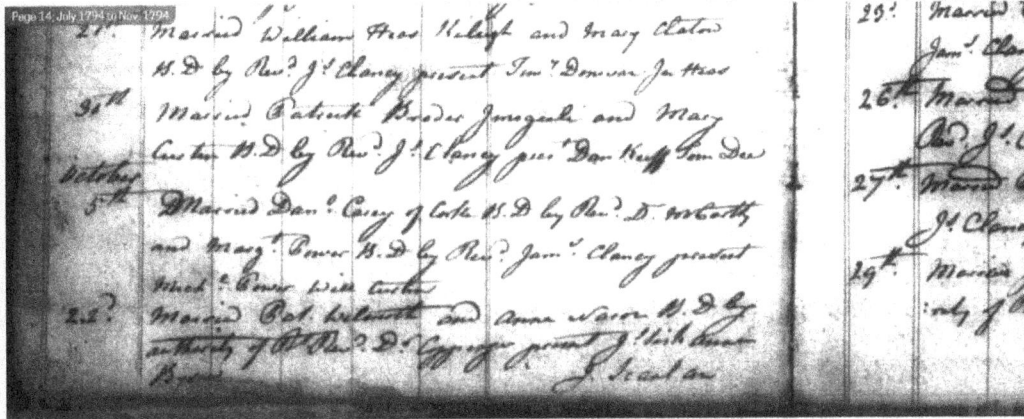

Cloyne Parish Microfilm - Irish Marriages:
Pat Wilmoth and Anne Nason; October 23(?), 1794

Catholic church baptism records show that Patrick Wilmott and Ann Nason had three children: Patrick, Michael, and Ann. All were baptized as Roman Catholic at address: W Well, Parish/District: Aghada, Ireland. (Note: The W Well listed as the address on all three of the children's birth transcriptions may refer to a location associated with a Holy Well, which are plentiful in County Cork.) [15] According to church baptismal records Patrick Wilmott was baptized on December 16, 1801 (sponsors were Thomas Callahan and Joan Keefe); Michael Wilmot was baptized on July 28, 1803 (sponsors were James Hanning and Mary Curtin); and, Ann Wilmott was baptized on January 8, 1806 (sponsors were William Ahern and Anastatia Sullivan).[16] At this time, the ancestral search is ongoing regarding further background information on both parents, Patrick and Ann(e).

---

[15] W Well appears on Patrick's birth transcription record of 1801, Michael's birth transcription record of 1803 and on Ann's birth transcription record of 1806. "Although puzzling, I think this may refer to a location associated with a Holy Well, which are plentiful in Co. Cork." Walsh, Michael. (2018). MAGI Family Lines. (Independent research for Keith Wilmot). https://www.michael@myirishconnections.com.

[16] Church Baptism Records. (2017). *Mallow Heritage Centre* (Cork North and East). Retrieved from https://www.rootsireland.ie. The Aghada parish is one of 46 parishes within the Cloyne Diocese, County Cork. Note: Baptism records are only an approximate estimate for date and place of birth.

Great-Great Grandfather, Michael Wilmott
Church Baptism Record

## 1800s Historic Note:

In 1800, some four and one-half million people lived in Ireland. By the autumn of 1845, when the Great Famine struck Ireland, there were more than eight million inhabitants. Today there is approximately 4.9 million inhabitants in Ireland and approximately 1.8 million people in Northern Ireland. At the beginning of the 19th century, the Acts of Union 1800 comes into effect which united the Kingdom of Ireland with Great Britain, forming the United Kingdom of Great Britain and Ireland. Years later, Northern Ireland and the Irish Free State were established in 1921.

In Europe, the French Revolution had come to an end in 1799 and Napoleon rose to prominence during the Napoleonic Wars (1803-1815). In the United States, approximately a quarter of a century after the American Revolution, Thomas Jefferson had been elected President in 1801, the Louisiana Purchase acquisition followed in 1803 which in turn led to the Lewis and Clark expedition in1804, the precursor to the great movement West.

# MICHAEL WILMOT

## (2ⁿᵈ Great Grandfather, Abt July 1803 - 1867)

Currently, our research acknowledges that there is a gap in documentation for Michael from the time of his 1803 baptismal in Ireland up to his documented marriage to Mary Collan on April 29, 1830 (although the search is ongoing). Their marriage was a catholic wedding which took place at St-Jean Bureau de Sante (Saint John Board of Health), Acadie (Nova Scotia and New Brunswick), Canada. The wedding certificate record indicated Michael Wilmot as son of Patrick Wilmot and Anne 'Nation' of Cloyne, County Cork, Ireland. Mary Collan was listed as the daughter of John Collan and Eleanor Mullin from a parish in Urney, County Tyrone, Ireland.[17] If the Roman Catholic baptismal records are correct, Michael would have likely been in his mid to late twenties when he emigrated to St. John, New Brunswick, Canada (baptized in 1803, Aghada, Ireland; married in 1830, St. John, New Brunswick). There is no record of when or how Michael and Mary met prior to their marriage or how and why they traveled to Canada. And at this time, there is no confirmed history of Mary Collan, her father John Collan, or her mother Eleanor Mullin, other than what is noted on the referenced wedding certificate.

The question remains, however; why did Michael (and Mary for that matter) leave Ireland prior to 1830? We do know that years prior to 1830 were a period of unrest in Ireland. After the Napoleonic Wars ended in 1815, the British Isles were thrust into a time of deep economic and agricultural depression which led to much social upheaval and class conflict in Ireland. Between 1815 and 1830, several detrimental events occurred, e.g., the great fever epidemic of 1816-1819,[18] Irish famines in both 1816-1817 and 1821-1822,[19] along with economic class injustices which were felt by the Irish rural world of the landless and land-poor tenants, e.g., issues of high rents and tithes. Together these concerns created an atmosphere of despair as unsettled grievances throughout Ireland. As a result, the great 'Rockite' movement of 1821-1824 began. This was a violent agrarian rebellion movement which was fueled by a combination of economic, sectarian (Protestant versus Catholic), and political motives. The Rockite movement resorted to both murder

---

[17] Acadia, Canada, Vital and Church Records. *Drouin Collection*, 1757-1946. (2007). Digital Images. Ancestry.com.

[18] "One of the worst disease outbreaks, in Irish terms, to make headlines was a typhus fever epidemic in the early 19th century. Between 1816 and 1819, typhus racked up 1.5 million cases and killed about 65,000 people in Ireland, according to estimates, with the greatest rate of mortality recorded in the summer of 1817." Ruxton, D. (2020). Wakes, beggars and 'bad air': When typhus killed 65,000 people in Ireland. The Irish Times. Retrieved from https://www.irishtimes.com/news/ireland/irish-news/wakes-beggars-and-bad-air-when-typhus-killed-65-000-people-in-ireland-1.4203488.

[19] "This calamity of nature led to the horrendous subsistence crisis of 1822.....even in accessible regions it produced appalling misery and semistarvation among small farmers, cottiers, and laborers for five or six months." Donnelly, J. S. Jr. (2009). Captain Rock: The Irish Agrarian Rebellion of 1821-1824. The University of Wisconsin Press, page 56.

and incendiarism as weapons of warfare and consisted not only of the poor but better-off farmers as well which, "in short, showed little inclination to submit to control by Catholic priests or members of the landed elite and presented a stiff test to the Protestant Ascendancy in Ireland."[20]

The Rockite movement was an enormous challenge during this period which led to a 'scheme' of government assisted emigration to Canada in the early 1820s. "The scheme was aimed at precisely those areas of north Cork where agrarian violence became most intense, and the principal goal, especially in the minds of the local landowners involved, was to rid themselves of some of the worst troublemakers on their estates."[21] The idea was that the first movement of emigrants would eventually turn into a mass movement of emigrants to follow. The idea became a reality when in 1823, a total of 568 emigrants sailed from Cork on two ships to Upper Canada. The experiment was led by Bathurst's deputy, Robert Wilmot Horton,[22] and the attorney general for Upper Canada, John Beverly Robinson. The first experiment was a success and by 1825, fifty thousand applicants had signed up for the next round of government-assisted emigration. Subsequently, 2,024 of the 50,000 applicants were selected and they set sail from Cork in nine ships arriving at the city of Quebec in the summer of 1825. However, in time, emigration from Ireland without government assistance greatly increased due to the repeal of all restrictions on emigration from Britain and Ireland in 1827 which, in turn, resulted in lower fares.[23] The government assisted emigration scheme of 1823 and 1825 probably had little effect on the Rockite movement but it did lead to a surge in emigration after 1827 to the U.S. and Canada. Obviously, Michael ended up in St. John, New Brunswick. When, why or how we do not know, but we are aware of the hostile environment in and around County Cork where he lived prior to 1830. Whether his intent was to escape the hardships for adventure or a new life we have no idea, but we do know there were adequate opportunities in the timber industry, fisheries, and/or farming for him to pursue in Atlantic Canada.

---

[20] Donnelly, J.S. Jr., page 4.
[21] Donnelly, J.S., Jr., p. 327.
[22] The only son of Sir Robert Wilmot, baronet of Osmaston, Derbyshire, was well known for advocating that poor British and Irish individuals emigrate to the colonies and be granted land there. In 1806 he married Anne Beatrix, co-heiress of Eusebius Horton of Catton, Derbyshire, and upon his father-in-law's will at time of death, assumed by Royal license the surname Horton. Thus, he became known as Sir Robert Wilmot-Horton. Australian Dictionary of Biography, Volume I. (1966). Sir Robert Wilmot Horton (1784-1841). Retrieved from http://adb.anu.edu.au/biography/horton-sir-robert-wilmot-2199.
[23] Donnelly, J.S., Jr., p. 334.

## Historic Note:

From a historical perspective, between the end of the Napoleonic Wars in 1815 and the 1840s, half a million Irish arrived in Canada, and during this time, the Irish were Canada's principal colonizers. Interestingly, for nearly a century the Irish had left their native country in search of a better life that 'Atlantic' Canada offered. Few were compelled by force or famine to leave Ireland - they deliberately chose to emigrate. However, as the 19th century progressed, with Ireland's ever-growing population and periods of economic and agricultural depression, Irish laborers sought the Atlantic region where the demand for labor brought higher wages than was possible in Ireland. The timber trade became the impetus between New Brunswick and Ireland for both emigration and economic development. The ports of Londonderry and Cork traded regularly with New Brunswick, offering space in their vessels for immigrants as they set off to cross the Atlantic to collect timber cargoes. Later, Irish Catholics would seek work in New Brunswick's lumber camps seeking a better life in the New World. In New Brunswick, Saint John's Irish Catholics primarily originated from counties in Ulster (which includes County Tyrone - Mary Collan's home county as recorded on the marriage certificate) and County Cork (similarly noted as Michael's home county).[24] Thus, the flourishing timber trade provided an inexpensive means for the immigrant to cross the Atlantic - perhaps the method Michael and Mary chose. Michael and Mary may or may not have escaped the perils of Partridge Island located in the Harbor of St. John. Partridge Island was an inspection station established in 1816, (similar to Ellis Island but 76 years earlier), where ships with disease and sick passengers aboard were required to stop and subsequently, both the ship and passengers were placed in quarantine for follow up inspection by medical staff. The ships were fumigated and those individuals who were sick, were exposed to kerosene showers followed by hot showers and steam cleaning of all clothing. The individuals who did not survive the quarantine were buried on the island.[25]

After Michael and Mary's marriage in St. John they proceeded to have seven children, five of which were born Catholic, in St. John, New Brunswick, Canada, and two were born in Manhattan, New York. Baptismal records for four of the five children born in Canada are listed below:[26]

1. James Wilmott (great grandfather), 1831-1874, was born of the lawful marriage of Michael Wilmott and Mary 'Collin' and baptized on April 26, 1831, age one day. James was

---

[24] Camey, L. H., (2016). Atlantic Canada's Irish Immigrants, A Fish and Timber Story. Dundurn Press, p. 28-32.
[25] Campy, p. 186-187.
[26] Acadia, Canada, Vital and Church Records. *Drouin Collection.* 1757-1946.

baptized by John Carroll and the sponsor was Margaret McWilliams. (*See* below baptismal record for James Wilmott).

2. William Wilmott, 1833-1857, the son of Michael Wilmott and Mary 'Collins', baptized on November 1, 1835, age two years. Sponsors were noted as James Mansfield and Mary Bithele.

3. Ellen Wilmott was born about 1837, no baptismal record.

4. Alice "Ally" Wilmott, 1838-1928, the daughter of Michael Wilmott and Mary 'Collins', was baptized on or about December 9, 1838, age five weeks.

5. Mary Ann Wilmott, 1841- after 1880, the daughter of Michael Wilmott and Mary 'Collins', was baptized on March 21, 1841, age, eight days.

6. Peter Wilmot was born about 1844 in Manhattan, New York, and died August 22, 1892, Manhattan, New York.

7. John Wilmot was born about 1847, Manhattan, New York, and died at age 61, on or about April 18, 1901, and buried in Calvary Cemetery, New York, April 19, 1901.

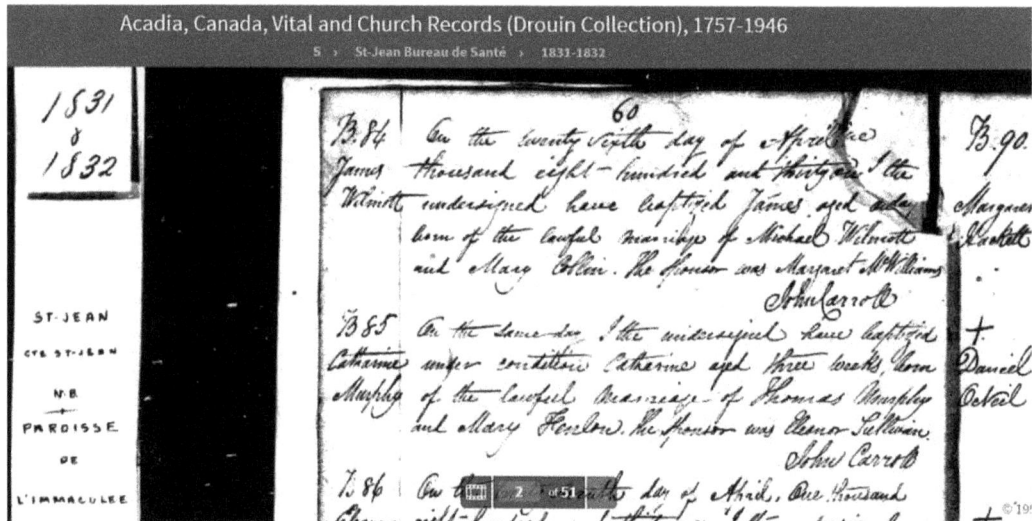

James Wilmott Baptismal Record - 1831 – St. John, New Brunswick

Currently, there is no further information on Michael and Mary's life in St. John, New Brunswick. However, in approximately 1844, after living ten or more years in St. John, New Brunswick, Canada, they moved to Manhattan, New York, with their five children. Around their time of arrival in Manhattan, Michael and Mary had their sixth child, Peter. Five years later came John, the seventh child. The 1840s had to be a trying time for Michael and Mary having decided to relocate during an era of surging immigration to St. John, New York City, Boston, and other coastal cities not only by the Irish but by many European immigrants. The question remains, why did Michael and Mary move? Many immigrants passed through St. John, New Brunswick, in the 1840s as previously noted, however, most did not stay and moved on to other parts of Canada or the United States. Although we do not know exactly where Michael and Mary may have lived in St. John, we do know that a large group of Irish-speaking Irish Catholics from Cork, Ireland, clustered in York Point, Kings Ward, St. John, making this perhaps the most exclusive residential concentration of poor Irish Catholics in the city.[27] York Point was located at the north end of Kings Ward, a district of wharfs and tenements on the ward's west side near the St. John river. Housing and job markets were being affected by sectarian violence as new immigrants arrived in the early 1840s. As Gordon W. Winder explains:

Sectarian violence between the Orange Order and Irish-Catholics tore apart Saint John in the 1840s. While the conflict emerged from transplanted antipathies and traditions of violence, it resulted in specific local clashes in Saint John. To a large extent, this violence centered on the Irish Catholic ghetto at York Point. Orange Order parades through York Point met with violence, and groups on both sides resorted to vandalism, arson, assaults, and riots. These sectarian clashes, which also included resistance to measures imposed by authorities, carried the hallmarks of pre-industrial social violence. At the same time, these were public and political acts imbued with ritual, drama, and publicity, and they involved struggles to define the community identity within a changing urban terrain.[28]

Whether this upheaval was the catalyst for Michael and Mary's departure we do not know, but it is a possibility. Another possibility was the beleaguered labor market for Irish Catholics who found little foothold in trades such as ship building, coopering and metal working trades. However, one trade which predominately stood out for the Irish Catholics during this time-period was that of 'cartman'. In 1837 there were only 40 cartmen in Kings Ward, by 1851 there were 83. Approximately eighty percent of the cartmen were either Irish Catholic or Irish Protestant. This was obviously a contested trade at the time, with most of the Irish cartmen arriving by 1840 or before.[29] Perhaps the congested cartman trade was a reason Michael left as this was his main trade upon moving to Manhattan where he lived and worked next to the wharves and slips along the East River. In sum, although some conjecture, the sectarian violence and the contested labor market may have been reason to re-locate to New York.

---

[27] Winder, G. W. (2000). Trouble in the North End: The Geography of Social Violence in Saint John 1840-1860. *Acadiensis*, Vol. 29, No. 2 Spring, 2000. pp. 27-57.
[28] Winder, G.W., p. 1.
[29] Winder, G.W., p. 20.

# JAMES WILMOT - (Great Grandfather, 1831-1874)

The following section will merge Michael Wilmot(t)'s (2nd Great Grandfather) and James Wilmot(t)'s (Great Grandfather) story after their arrival in Manhattan, New York, and continue to their time of death.

## The 1830s

James Wilmott (Wilmot), our great grandfather, the first child of Michael and Mary, was born April 25, 1831, in St John, New Brunswick, Canada. James was baptized Catholic on April 26, 1831, according to the de l'Immaculee Conception's records located at the St-Jean Bureau de Sante (St. John's Bureau of Health), Acadie (Nova Scotia and New Brunswick).[30] At this time, there is no additional chronological Canadian documentation until at age 11, when James was identified with his mother Mary 'Wilmouth', age 30,[31] and four siblings (William, age 9; Ellen, age 6; Ellis (Alice), age 3; and Mary Ann, age 1) having departed St. George, New Brunswick on the ship *Flora* arriving in Boston, Massachusetts on June 21, 1842. (*see* below)[32] The time sequence for Mary and her children to travel to and eventually settle in New York with Michael is uncertain. However, Michael (great-great grandfather), on November 2, 1844, signed a declaration petition in the Court of Common Pleas for the City and County of New York signifying his "bona fide intention to become a Citizen of the United States." (*see* below)[33] This document establishes a tentative baseline for the settlement of Michael Wilmot's family in New York City. (Note: There is also documentation for the Court of Common Pleas which shows a signed declaration petition for Michael Wilmott on November 2, 1846).

Michael and Mary's family arrived in Manhattan, New York, during a time of surging immigration by the Irish, primarily those trying to escape the drought and famine conditions in their homeland. The conditions in Manhattan during this time frame was extremely distressing with overcrowding, tenement housing, poverty, sickness, and crime (not much different from where they came).

---

[30] St-Jean Bureau de Sante, 1831-1832. Acadia, Canada, Vital and Church Records, *Drouin Collection*, 1752-1946. Digital Images. (2007). Ancestry.com.

[31] If the ship *Flora's* manifest was correct, having listed Mary's age as 30 in 1842 when the ship arrived in Boston, then Mary's approximate year of birth would have been approximately 1812.

[32] Massachusetts Passenger and Crew List, 1820-1946, for Mary Wilmouth, Roll M277, Arriving at Boston, MA, 1820-1891. Digital Images. (2006). Ancestry.com.

[33] Index to Petitions for Naturalizations Filed in Federal, State, and Local Courts in New York City, 1792-1906. Digital Images. (2013). Ancestry.com.

# Massachusetts, Passenger and Crew Lists, 1820-1963

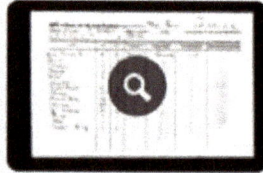

**View Image**

**View Record**

| | |
|---:|:---|
| **Name** | Mary Wilmouth |
| **Gender** | Female |
| **Age** | 30 |
| **Birth Date** | 1812 |
| **Departure Place** | St George, New Brunswick |
| **Arrival Date** | 21 Jun 1842 |
| **Arrival Place** | Boston, Massachusetts, USA |
| **Ship** | Flora |

Passenger List - Ship *Flora* - Mary Wilmouth and Family
St. George, New Brunswick to Boston, Massachusetts

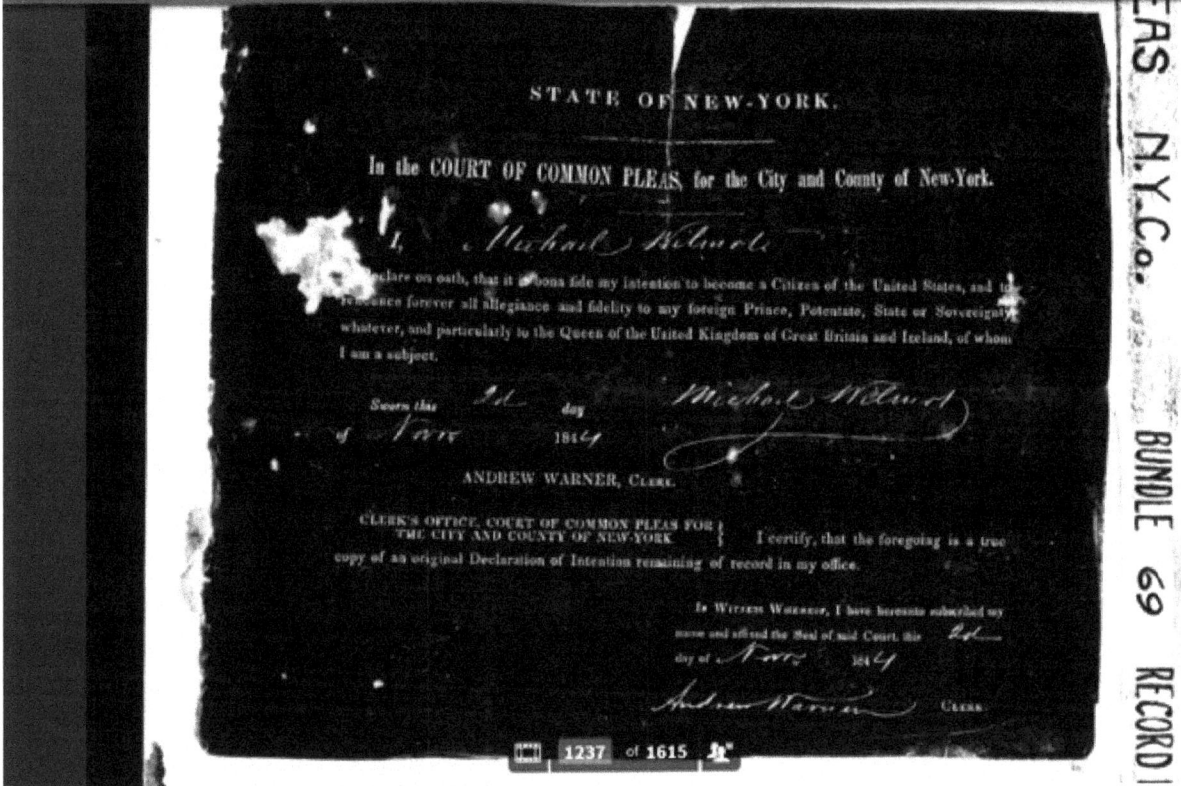

Michael Wilmot - Petition for Naturalization - 1844

## Manhattan, New York in the 1840s

The 1840s was a period of vast immigration to New York City by foreigners from abroad taking up refuge in lower Manhattan along the waterways of the East River on one side and the Hudson River on the other side. Charles Dickens describes the scene in Manhattan during his 1842 American tour, "…..that below the narrow thoroughfare of Wall Street, the Stock Exchange and Lombard Street of New York, on the water-side, where the bowsprits of ships stretch across the footway, and almost thrust themselves into the windows, lie the noble American vessels which have made their Packer Service the finest in the world. They have brought hither the foreigners who abound in all the streets: not, perhaps, that there are more here, than in other commercial cities; but elsewhere, they have particular haunts, and you must find them out; here, they pervade the town." [34]

Charles Dickens continued to tour lower Manhattan in 1842 with two policemen and while doing so, Dickens described the cultural and environmental setting of an area referred to as Five Points, Sixth Ward, Manhattan, New York.[35] A general description by Dickens of the Five Points is as follows:

What place is this, to which the squalid street conducts us?

Poverty, wretchedness, and vice, are rife enough where we are going now…..[T]his is the place: these narrow ways, diverging to the right and left, and reeking everywhere with dirt and filth. Such lives are led here, bear the same fruits here as elsewhere. The coarse and bloated faces at the doors, have counterparts at home, and all the wide world over.

Debauchery has made the very houses prematurely old. See how the rotten beams are tumbling down, and how the patched and broken windows seem to scowl dimly, like eyes that have been hurt in drunken fray.

A kind of square of leprous houses, some of which are attainable only by crazy wooden stairs without. What lies behind this tottering flight of steps, that creak beneath our tread? – a miserable room, lighted by one dim candle, and destitute of all comfort, save that which may be hidden in a wretched bed. Beside it, sits a man his elbows on his knees: his forehead hidden in his hands. What ails that man? asks the foremost officer. 'Fever,' he sullenly replies, without looking up. Conceive the fancies of a feverish brain, in such a place as this![36]

---

[34] Dickens, C., (2006). American Notes for General Circulation. Internet Archive: Echo Library, Teddington, Middlesex, p. 60. (Reprint, original published in London, 1850).

[35] Five Points (or The Five Points) was a 19th-century neighborhood in Lower Manhattan, New York City. The neighborhood was generally defined as being bound by Centre Street to the west, the Bowery to the east, Canal Street to the north, and Park Row to the south.

[36] Dickens, C., p. 65-66.

## 1840s Historic Note:

In 1840 more than half of the persons over ten years of age who died in New York City were immigrants, mainly Irish and Germans who lived in unsanitary tenement dwellings. A typhus outbreak occurred in 1842 and a cholera epidemic between 1848-1849, killed 5,071 in New York City.[37]

In 1840 New York City had a population of 327,000, in 1850 the population surged to 590,000 (a 55.4% increase). Also, during this time, the New York City Police Department, NYPD, was established May 23, 1845. During the 1840s, three United States presidents were elected: William Henry Harrison, 1840; James K. Polk, 1844; and General Zachary Taylor, 1848.

## The 1850s

In 1850, the United States census listed Michael Wilmott and his entire family (Michael and Mary and their seven children) as living in Dwelling 626, Seventh Ward, Manhattan, New York. Both Michael and Mary were recorded as being 45 years of age and from Ireland. According to the census, Mary could not read or write at the time of the census. The 1850 census indicates that James (great grandfather) was 17 years old and born in New Brunswick. Michael and James were working as 'laborers' during this time. Four of the children, Ann - age 12, Alice - age 10, Mary - age 8, and Peter - age 5, all had attended school during the past year. William - age 15, was listed as having neither an occupation nor having attended school. As noted in the census, the Wilmott family lived in dwelling 626, Seventh Ward (Manhattan), New York City, New York. According to a survey map of Manhattan in 1852, dwelling 626 of the Seventh Ward was located on Water Street between Gouverneur Street and Scamel Street in lower east side Manhattan, two blocks west of the Gouverneur Slip located on the East River (Gouverneur Street was named after Abraham Gouverneur a French immigrant who became a merchant and political activist; Scamel Street is most likely named after Revolutionary War hero Alexander Scamel). The Gouverneur Slip was the docking and transit site for the ferry to Hudson Avenue, Brooklyn, New York.[38]

During the surge of immigrants in the 1850s, the Irish population accounted for approximately 38 percent of those inhabitants in the Second, Fourth, and Seventh wards facing the East River. These wards served as a distribution point for thousands of refugees from Ireland and

---

[37] Ernst, R. (1994). Immigrant Life in New York City, 1825-1863. Syracuse University Press, Syracuse, New York., pages 52-53.

[38] Library of Congress. (2017). Map of City, New York, Extending North to Fiftieth Street. Surveyed and Drawn by John F. Harrison, C.E. Published by M. Dripps, 103 Fulton Street and 50 Ann Street, NY, 1852. Retrieved from https://www.loc.gov/item/2017586293/.

the easy ferriage across the river to Brooklyn which extended an Irish population to an area less constricted by land speculation in Manhattan.[39] (Observation: This had to have been a difficult time for the 'Wilmott' family with seven children all living in small tenement quarters. Michael's wage as a laborer was probably a mere pittance for his family's support).

By 1853, James had met Sophia Kline (or Cline) and they were married on September 4, 1853, in Manhattan, New York.[40] Sophia was 15 at the time of marriage and James 21.[41] They were married by a Justice of the Peace and the two witnesses at the time of marriage were John Terry and Mrs. Kline (Sophia's mother?). The church where James and Sophia were married is likely the Methodist Episcopalian Church which was located on 9 Willet Street between Grand Street and Broome Street in Manhattan's Thirteenth Ward (*see* photo below).[42] This location was approximately five blocks North from dwelling 626 located on Water Street directly adjacent to Manhattan's Seventh Ward (Michael Wilmot's family dwelling). At the time, Manhattan's Thirteenth Ward, in addition to the Tenth and Eleventh wards, formed the nucleus of "*Kleindeutschland*" or Little Germany, the center of German business activity. During this time-period the New York German and Irish populations together surpassed the total number of individuals of all other nationalities combined.

---

[39] Ernst, R., page 40 (*see* citation 26, Chapter 4).

[40] NYC: Willett Street Church Baptism and Marriage Records. New York and Vicinity, United Methodist Church Records, 1775-1949. Digital Image. Ancestry.com.

[41] United States Marriages Transcription. Sophia Kline and James Wilmot. Digital Images. Findmypast.com. FamilySearch film number: 001671673.

[42] The Bialystoker Synagogue at 7-11 Bialystoker Place, formerly Willett Street, between Grand and Broome Streets in the Lower East Side neighborhood of Manhattan, New York City is an Orthodox Jewish synagogue. The building was constructed in 1826 as the Willett Street Methodist Episcopal Church; the synagogue purchased the building in 1905. The synagogue was designated a New York City Landmark in 1966. It is one of only four early-19th century fieldstone religious buildings surviving from the late Federal period in Lower Manhattan, and is the oldest building used as a synagogue in New York City. *See* Willett Street Methodist Episcopal Church. Retrieved from http://daytoninmanhattan.blogspot.com/2015/06/the-1826-willetts-street-methodist.html.

The Bialystoker Synagogue formerly known as the Willett Street Methodist Episcopal Church

In 1855, New York held their own census. The State of New York took a census every ten years from 1825 to 1875.[43] The 1855 census taken on June 25, 1855, lists James and Sophia Wilmott as family 256 living in dwelling 44 (a brick building possibly on Broome Street), the Sixth Election District, Thirteenth Ward of New York County (Manhattan), New York. According to the 1855 census, James was age 23, male, born in New Brunswick, married, a resident of the city for 14 years, his occupation was noted as 'Truckman',[44] and he was a naturalized voter. Sophia was listed as 17, female, wife, born in New York, married and she claimed residence in the city

---

[43] 1855 State of New York Census, June 22, 1855, Sixth Election District, Thirteenth Ward, New York County. Note: In addition, the State of New York took a census in 1892 and then every ten years from 1905 to 1925. New York County (Manhattan) is missing from most New York censuses; however, it is included in the 1855, 1905, 1915 and 1925 censuses.

[44] Throughout this research, truckman, cartman, and carman will be noted interchangeably in various census reports. Essentially the terms denote haulers of commodities using a single horse and a two-wheeled cart. The cartmen, although unskilled workers, were one of the most important labor groups in American cities. The forerunners of the Teamsters Union, the cartmen's culture and their relationship with New York's municipal government are the direct ancestors of the city's fabled taxicab drivers. For further discussion *see* Hodges, G. R. (2012). New York City Cartmen, 1667-1850. New York: University Press.

for 17 years and born in (New York?). Also living as family 256 at dwelling 44 with James and Sophia were James' brother William, age 22, and his wife Margaret, age 19. William was noted as being born in New Brunswick and like James, a 'Truckman,' a naturalized voter, and a resident of New York for 14 years. The census indicated that William's wife Margaret was born in Ireland and had lived in New York for nine years. Next door to James and Sophia in the same building, family 255, lived James' father and mother, Michael, and Mary Wilmott with three of James' siblings, Mary A. age 13, Peter age 11, and John age 7. All three siblings were listed as being born in New York. The 1855 census identified Michael as 44, male, married, born in Ireland, a resident of New York for 14 years, employed as a Truckman and a declared naturalized voter. Michael's wife Mary was reported as 42, married, born in Ireland and at the time, she had maintained a New York residence for 14 years as well.

The 1857 U.S. City Directory for New York City, New York, lists James Wilmot, 'carman', h. 327 Delancey Street (*see* Charles Klines' obituary referencing James' address as 327 Delancey Street). There was a Michael Wilmot listed as a 'porter, h. 827 Delancey Street', but uncertain if this is the same Michael Wilmot (2nd great grandfather).

On September 3, 1857, William Wilmott (our great uncle), James' brother, died at age 23 years, 6 months. According to the Department of Records and Information Services, William's address at death was 38 Lewis Street, Manhattan, New York, (located between Delancey Street and Broome Street approximately four blocks from the boat slips on the East River). His occupation at time of death was noted as Truck Driver. His place of birth was listed as New Brunswick. The records indicate William died from Phthisis, more commonly known as tuberculosis. He was buried in Calvary Cemetery September 4, 1857, one day after his death. A letter from Joseph Giulietti, Superintendent of Calvary Cemetery, stated that William was buried in grave-holding 2-26-N-6. Giulietti noted that this grave is a 'non-title' grave-holding and the property is owned by the cemetery. This essentially implies that William was probably indigent at the time and New York City likely paid for the expenses. No headstone can be erected because 'any other burials in this grave would be of no relation' which means this was a multiple burial site (*see* letter below). William's death precedes the interment of the Wilmott's grave-holding 4-13-D-15 at Calvary Cemetery (*see* Photo, page 40). Interestingly, the United States Army, Register of Enlistments for the period October 1850 through December 1854,[45] list William Wilmot as having enlisted in the Army March 3, 1853. His physical description indicated that he was age 21, 5'8", blue eyes, sandy hair, fair complexion and born in St. John, New Brunswick. His occupation at the time of enlistment state 'Soldier' having been recruited by Captain Howe in New York. Unfortunately, the records note that William deserted the Army on August 8, 1853. (Note: During these hard times in Manhattan, the possibility existed that William may have engaged in 'bounty - jumping', the widespread practice of enlisting, collecting the cash bonus, deserting, reenlisting,

---

[45] U.S. Army Register of Enlistments, 1798-1914. Digital Images. Ancestry.com.

collecting another bonus, etc., which was an inherent defect in the system in early U.S. history…..from the time of the French and Indian Wars up to the Civil War.)[46]

May 20, 2020

Keith A. Wilmot
4002 Deep River
San Antonio, TX 78253

Re: 2-26-N-6

Dear Mr. Wilmot,

Please be advised that William Wilmott, 23 years and 6 months old, was buried in the above described grave holding on September 4, 1857. However, this is a non-title grave holding. This property is owned by the cemetery. There is no headstone on this grave and none can be placed there. Any other burials in this grave would be on no relation.

I trust that this information proves helpful and we are pleased to have been of assistance.

Very truly yours,

Joseph Giulietti
Superintendent

JG:sb

## The Trustees of St. Patrick's Cathedral - Calvary Cemetery - William Wilmott

---

[46] Encyclopedia Britannica. (2019). Bounty System. Retrieved from https://www.britannica.com/event/Bounty-System.

## 1850s Historic Note:

The United States Census of 1850 indicates a total population of 23,191,876, a 35.9% increase from a decade before. Over three million people now live in its most populous state, New York. Central Park in Manhattan, New York City, was established in 1857 and although a small portion of the park opened in 1858, construction continued to its current size of 843 acres, completed in 1873 (today it is New York City's 5th largest park). During the 1850s, three presidents were elected: Millard Filmore (1850-1853); Franklin Pierce (1853-1857); and James Buchanan (1857-1861). From August 21 to October 15, 1858 - a series of seven debates between politicians Stephen Douglas and Abraham Lincoln occur in Illinois.

## The 1860s

The 1860 United States Federal Census taken July 24, 1860, for Election District 1, Thirteenth Ward, New York (Manhattan), New York, shows James Wilmot age 28, employed as a carman (cartman) living in dwelling 266, family number 1005. James' place of birth was listed as New York. Dwelling 266 was an apartment consisting of four families located on Delancey Street approximately five blocks from the Delancey boat slip on the East River. Also listed as living at this dwelling was a female, Jane Wilmot, age 22; Alice age 11 months; and, Charles Klein, age 24, whose occupation was listed as 'Oysterman', and his place of birth was New York. It is uncertain what the relationship of Jane was to the household - she was noted as having been born in New York (this may be Jane McIntyre who James married in October of 1872 after Sophia's presumed death or, more likely, it could have been Sophia - in 1860 Sophia would have been 22 years of age). Sophia was not listed in this census which is somewhat odd since Alice, age 11 months, was James and Sophia's daughter. Charles Klein was James' brother-in-law or Sophia's brother (*see* below, Charles Klein's obituary from the New York Herald). Interestingly, family number 1004, living next to James in dwelling 266, was Francis Wilmot, age 56, and his wife Mary, age 55. Both Francis and Mary were from Ireland and Francis' occupation was that of a 'Truck Driver'. Living with Francis and Mary at this time were two boys, Peter, age 14, and John, age 11, both born in New York. It is likely that Peter and John were James' younger brothers; however, it is uncertain the relationship of Francis and Mary to James or his brothers.

On April 30, 1862, James Wilmott purchased the 'Wilmott' grave holding, 4-13-D-15, in Calvary Cemetery, Woodside, Queens, New York.[47] James purchased the cemetery plot in response to two deaths. James and Sophia's son James (age 6 months) died April 28, 1862, and Charles Kline (Klein) (age 26) died April 29, 1862. There are currently 11 burials in this grave

---

[47] Calvary Cemetery List of Interments in Section 4, Range 13, Plot D, Grave 15. Digital Images. (2017). Ancestry.com.

holding - beginning in 1862 and end as the final resting place for John Wilmott, James' brother, in 1901. Up until December 19, 2017, this grave holding was essentially an unmarked grave; however, on December 19, 2017, a headstone honoring the eleven individuals was placed by representatives of the Memorial Granite Corporation, Woodside, New York. The headstone was purchased and provided by the sons and daughter of Noble King Wilmot (*see* Photo, p. 40). The first person listed in burial sequence on the headstone was Charles Kline, age 26, who died on April 29, 1862. James and Sophia's son James who died at age 6 months, twenty-six days, was the second person listed having died April 28, 1862. Young James lived at 327 Delancey Street at time of death. To date, there is little information on son James other than he died from Hydrocephalus. Charles Kline, however, was the brother-in-law and brother of James and Sophia. Charles died from 'Consumption' (tuberculosis) according to the New York City death notice. The New York City death notice also indicated that Charles was born in New York and his attending physician was M. C. Tully, the same physician who attended young James.[48] The New York Herald listed Charles Cline's (Kline) obituary on May 1, 1862.[49] The obituary read as follows:

> Cline (Kline), On Tuesday, April 29, Charles Cline (Kline), aged 26 years, 3 months and 3 days. The relatives and friends of the family, the members of Jackson Fire Hose Co. No. 13, the members of Insurance Patrol No. 1, and the members of the Fire Department in general, are respectfully invited to attend the funeral, from the residence of his brother-in-law, James Wilmot, No. 327 Delancey Street, this (Thursday) afternoon, at two o'clock. His remains will be taken to Calvary Cemetery for interment.

In 1862, the New York City Fire Department was still a volunteer department and it appears that Charles had had quite an influence with the New York City fire department members as seen by the inclusive invitation to the funeral for 'all members' of the Fire Department and the Insurance Patrol in the obituary. An interesting note is that 327 Delancey Street (James and Sophia's address) was across the street from the Jackson Hose Company which was on the corner of Delancey Street and Mangin Street two blocks from the East River. (Note: The Jackson Hose Co. was originally organized February 7, 1844. It was located at 34 Mangin Street along the East River. As of November 1, 1865, after New York City terminated the volunteer fire department system, the Jackson Hose Company was officially disbanded as were all the other various volunteer hose companies in the city.)[50]

---

[48] Charles Kline. Death Notice. (2018). New York City Department of Records and Information Services. Municipal Archives: New York, NY.

[49] Charles Cline Obituary. (1862, May 1). New York Herald, page 5. New York, NY: 1840-1920.

[50] Costello, A.E. (1997). Our Firemen - A History of the New York Fire Departments, Volunteer and Paid. New York: Knickerbocker Press, pages 645 and 816.

# Historic Note: Insurance Patrols aka: New York City Fire Patrols[51]

The Insurance Patrol was a unique organization that worked closely with the New York Fire Department. Interestingly, the Insurance Patrol referenced in the obituary was officially known as the New York Fire Patrol and was a separate entity from the New York Fire Department. The New York Fire Patrol can be traced back to the American Revolution when it was known as the Hand-in Hand Fire Company organized for the sole purpose of conducting salvage operations in the old city of Manhattan. In 1839, the New York Fire Patrol was organized and operated by the New York Board of Fire Underwriters. The function was twofold: to discover fires and to prevent losses to insured properties. In 1853 the New York Board of Fire Underwriters was reorganized and became the Board of Fire Insurance Companies. As recorded in their minutes, "The Patrol shall aid the fire department in preserving the exposed property by covering the same with oiled cloths, by removal or otherwise so as most effectively protect the same from damage." In other words, the goal was to reduce insurance claims by protecting property and save owner's livelihoods. In 1867, the New York Fire Patrol was chartered by the state to legally extinguish fires and conduct salvage operations in New York City. The New York Fire patrol was in operation up until 2006 at such time that it was officially disbanded ending the last of the Insurance salvage corps in the United States. (Neither Charles Kline nor James Wilmot worked for the fire patrol; however, Charles as a volunteer fireman and James, most likely a paid fireman, would have worked closely with members of the various Insurance Patrols.)

Neither Michael nor Mary Wilmot's[52] listing has been found in either the federal census (1860) or the State of New York census (1865); however, there is evidence that Michael was alive up to 1867.[53] More specifically, Michael's death certificate confirms that he died on May 28, 1867, at his home, 26 Broome Street, 13th Ward, New York City (*see* death certificate below). The Coroner, William Schirmer viewed the body on May 29, 1867, at Michael's home and determined the cause of death as 'Rheumatism of the Heart'. The death certificate notes that at the time of death, Michael was married (most likely Mary was still alive at this time), age 57, his occupation was listed as Cartman, he had been a resident of New York City (Manhattan) for twenty-two years, and both his parents were born in Ireland. Michael was buried in Calvary Cemetery, Queens, New York, on May 30, 1867, in the same grave holding as James (6 months) and Charles Kline.[54] The

---

[51] Reagan, T.E. (2005). Images of America - New York Fire Patrol. Arcadia Publishing.
[52] Mary Wilmot's time, place, and cause of death are currently unknown.
[53] Michael Wilmot. New York City Death Notices Transcription, 1835-1880. Digital Images. Findmypast.com.
[54] Calvary List of Interments (*see* Photo, p. 40).

New York Herald listed Michael Wilmot's obituary on May 30, 1867.[55] The obituary read as follows:

> Willmott – Suddenly, on Tuesday, May 28, Michael Willmott, a native of Cloyne, County Cork, Ireland, aged 57 years and 9 months. The relatives and friends of the family are respectfully invited to attend his funeral, from his late residence, 26 Broome Street, this (Thursday) afternoon, at two o'clock. The remains will be taken to Calvary Cemetery for interment.

---

[55] Michael Wilmott Obituary. (1867, May 30). New York Herald, page 12. New York, NY: 1840-1920. Digital Images. Library of Congress, Washington, D.C.

Michael Wilmot Death Certificate - Municipal Archives
New York Department of Records and Information Services

## 1860s Historic Note:

In 1861 the American Civil War begins at Fort Sumpter and ends in 1865 when General Robert E. Lee surrenders at the Appomattox Court House. The Brooklyn Bridge, 1869 - 1883, was the world's first steel-wire suspension bridge and the first fixed crossing across the East River (*see* Print below). During the 1860s, three presidents were elected: Abraham Lincoln (1861-1865); Andrew Johnson, (1865-1869); Ulysses S. Grant (1869-1877).

Interestingly, after Abraham Lincoln's assassination on April 14, 1865, a procession carrying his body was solemnly paraded through the streets of Manhattan, New York City on April 26, 1865. The undertaker for President Lincoln was Peter Relyea who had once been the sexton for the Willett Street Methodist Episcopal Church (the church where James and Sophia were married). The procession proceeded up Broadway in Manhattan on its long journey to President Lincoln's final burial in Springfield, Illinois.

NEW YORK,

Bird's eye panoramic view print of Manhattan in 1873, looking north.
The Hudson River is on the west to the left. The Brooklyn Bridge (to the right) across the East River
was under construction from 1870 until 1883.
George Schlegel (Artist), George Degen (Publisher).

# The 1870s

The 1870 United States census taken June 14, 1870, for Election District 10, 13th Ward of New York City (Manhattan), identified James 'Willmot,' age 34, living in dwelling 42, family number 249, with his wife Sophia, age 32, and two children, William, age 7, and Alles (Alice), age 11. It is important to note that James and Sophia had a son, James, who died April 28, 1862, at six months and twenty-six days, and subsequently buried in Calvary Cemetery, (*See* Photo page 40). (Young James was not yet born for the 1860 census and died before the 1870 census). Young James' death notice indicated he died from hydrocephalus, which is the buildup of too much cerebrospinal fluid in the brain.[56] They also had another son, James A. - grandfather - who was born on or about August 28, 1870, shortly after the 1870 US census was taken in June of that year. According to this census, two other family members were living at the same dwelling with James and Sophia. The first was Mary, age 46, born in Ireland with both parents listed as being of foreign birth (this may likely have been James' mother since his father Michael died in 1867; however, the age for Mary, if recorded correctly, would have been 56). The second person was John, age 23, James' brother. Both James and John were employed as a 'carman' (cartman). Although James was recorded as being born in New York, both boxes for father and mother being foreign born were checked 'yes'.

Ironically, James Wilmott and family were included in another 1870 United States census for New York. This census was taken on January 7, 1870, for the 2nd District, 13th Ward, New York City, New York. On page 48 of the census, dwelling 33 (Lewis Street), James Wilmott and family are listed again. James Wilmott, male, 34, Cartman; Sophia, female, age 33; Alice, female, age 11; William, male, age 8; and, James, male, 6 months. All were noted as having been born in New York. Evidently, James and family moved during the time the 1870 census was being taken and obviously no contingency plan was in place for individuals who moved within the city during the census year.

Further review of the 1870 United States census for New York found the listing for James' sister Mary Ann who was now married to Joseph J. Lake, age 34, born in New York and who worked as a seaman. Mary and Joseph were listed as family 267, dwelling 43, the 10th District, 13th Ward, New York City, New York. In addition, James' sister Alice was now married to John C. Madara, age 39, who was born in New York and worked as a carman. Alice and John were listed as family 173, dwelling 41, the 12th District, 13th Ward, New York City, New York. And as referenced above, John, James' brother, was living with both James and Sophia in 1870. The dwellings of James (33 and 42), Alice (41), and Mary (43) during the 1870 census period were all located on Broome Street a few blocks from the Broome Street slip located on East Street along

---

[56] James Wilmott (b). Death Notice. New York City Department of Records and Information Services. Municipal Archives: New York, NY.

the East River. In addition, the 1870 U.S. census shows Peter 'Willmot', James' brother, age 30, employed as a Watchman, living with his wife, Margaret, age 28, at dwelling 340, Delancey Street (a block from Broome Street). Also listed as living with Peter and Margaret, was Mary, age 50, born in Ireland. This is probably our great-great grandmother, Michael's wife, however, the age is listed wrong - it probably should be age 70.[57] Also, in 1870, Ellen, James's sister, was married to George M. Warburton and she was possibly living in Rahway, New Jersey at the time.

Between the birth of James A. Wilmot in August of 1870[58] and October of 1872, James A.'s mother and James' wife, Sophia (great grandmother) passed-away (see information below on Sophia's purported death on September 7, 1872). Soon after Sophia's death, on October 20, 1872, the Bureau of Records of Vital Statistics, Health Department of the City of New York, shows that James Wilmot married Jane McIntyre, certificate of marriage number 7093. The Return of the Marriage document indicates that James Wilmot of 276 Delancey (Thirteenth Ward), Manhattan, New York, was 35 years of age, worked at the Fire Department, his father's name was Michael Wilmot and his mother's maiden name was Mary Collin. Note: If James worked at the 'Fire Department' as stated, he was likely to have been a full-time employee of the Metropolitan Fire Department since the transition from a volunteer department to a paid department took place in New York City in 1865 by an Act of the New York State Legislature.[59]

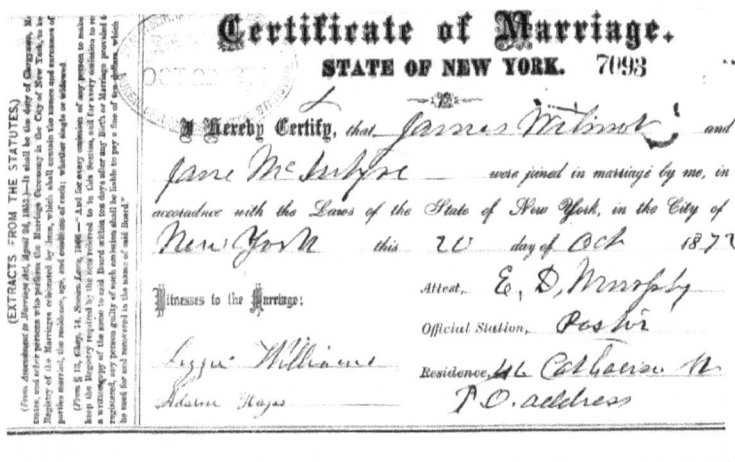

James Wilmot and Jane McIntyre - Certificate of Marriage

---

[57] The 1880 United States census also shows Mary Wilmot (Collan), great-great grandmother, living with Peter and Margaret Wilmot(t) as a 'boarder'. She was listed as 80 years of age. We have no further information for Mary and are uncertain as to either the time and place of death or her final burial site. (*see* Census Index, page 131).
[58] James A. Wilmot has several documented birth dates...... However, in the chronology of his life, the August 28, 1870 date appears to be the most likely birth date.
[59] Costello, A.E., page 810.

James Wilmot and Jane McIntyre's 'Return of a Marriage' - 1872

According to their 'Return of a Marriage' document, James' and Jane's place of residence at 276 Delancey in Manhattan's Thirteenth Ward was only a few blocks away from the East River and the Delancey 'boat slip.' Today, the Delancey boat slip has been replaced by the Williamsburg Bridge as a major transit route to Brooklyn. Prior to their marriage, Jane McIntyre had resided at 45 Cherry Street, Manhattan, New York. At the time of their marriage, Jane was listed as 25 years of age and her place of birth was recorded as New York City. Her fathers' name was listed as Robt (Robert) J. McIntyre and her mother's maiden name was Anna Trueman. Both James and Jane noted that this was their 'first' marriage. Witnesses included Lyzie Williams and Adeline Hayes.

Jane's listed address of 45 Cherry Street, located in Lower Manhattan's Fourth Ward, was just blocks from the East River near the transit location for the Catharine Ferry, a ferriage to the Main Street dock in Brooklyn. The Fourth Ward and specifically Cherry and Water Streets were directly adjacent to the Sixth Ward and the infamous 'Five Points' neighborhood characterized by a history of poor tenement housing, crime and gangs such as the 'Kerryonians' and the 'Dead Rabbits.'[60]

On August 15, 1874, less than two years after James married Jane McIntrye, James died from shock due to a fall from his wagon (ice cart). The tragic event occurred on the 'Ice Bridge' at the foot of Delancey Street, 'ER' (East River). (It is uncertain why the term 'Ice Bridge' was used since this was a phenomenon during cold winters in certain cold years in the 1800s in which ice floes would jam between Manhattan and Brooklyn allowing individuals to cross over the ice on foot as a substitute to ferry service). The place of inquest was 82 Canal Street, James' residence (NE corner of Canal Street and Greene Street). The death certificate, number 185845, noted that James was married, formerly a fireman and at time of death, an ice cart(man).[61] (It is likely that James, who was 'formerly a fireman' according to the death certificate, reverted to driving an ice cart due to his weakened state resulting from the onset of tuberculosis). A native of New Brunswick, James, at time of death, had lived in New York City for 30 years having immigrated to New York City (Manhattan) with his parents, Michael and Mary, both natives of Ireland. The coroner, Richard Croker, viewed the body on August 16, 1874, at James' residence and he officially declared the cause of death as phthisis pulmonalis (tuberculosis)[62] hastened by an accidental fall from his wagon on Delancey Street near the East River. The death certificate indicated that on August 17, 1874, James Wilmot was buried in Calvary Cemetery.[63] The August 17, 1874, edition of the New York Herald newspaper listed James' obituary. The obituary read as follows:

---

[60] Ernst, R., page 57.

[61] New York City was the nation's biggest consumer of ice; by mid-century, it was buying 285,000 tons of ice a year. Ice brought with it significant social and cultural changes. It helped keep meat, fish, and dairy products safe, improving both food quality and the public's health. The availability of ice meant that beer could be brewed and stored all year long; more than 120 breweries were up and running in Manhattan and Brooklyn by 1879. And ice was used medicinally, as hospitals dispensed it to fever victims to help lower body temperature. Rockland Lake and the Hudson Valley Ice Industry. https://hvmag.com/life-style/rockland-lake-and-the-hudson-valley-ice-industry/.

[62] Diseases such as tuberculosis and pneumonia were the major cause of death in New York City between 1860 and 1900. Intestinal bacterial maladies such as diarrhea, associated with high infant mortality was second. Cholera was the most feared. Kennedy, R.C. (2001). Harp Week. New York Times. https://archive.nytimes.com/www.nytimes.com/learning/general/onthisday/harp/0414.html.

[63] James Wilmot (a). New York City Death Certificate 185845. Department of Records and Information Services. Municipal Archives.

Wilmoth – In this city, on August 15th, Saturday, James Wilmoth, age 42. The relatives and friends are respectfully invited to attend the funeral from his late residence, 82 Canal Street, this day (Monday), at two o'clock.[64]

James Wilmot's Death Certificate - 185845 - New York City, New York

[64] James Wilmot Obituary. (1874, August 17). The New York Herald, page 6. Digital Images. Library of Congress, Washington, D.C.

Note: In the 30 years that James lived in Manhattan, he lived in approximately seven different locations, mostly in the 13th Ward on either Delancey Street or Broome Street near the East River. His parents and siblings seemed to do likewise.

It is also worth mentioning that within the time frame of James and Jane's short marriage, they had a son Peter who was born and died in 1874, age 3 days. It is uncertain if Peter died before or after James; however, both James and son Peter were buried at Calvary Cemetery in the same year and same grave. (*See* the below grave-holding, page 40). Also, during that year, the 1874 U.S. City Directories for Paterson, New Jersey, shows that Jane Wilmott, a widow, was living at 122 Maple in Paterson.[65] Evidently, Jane moved to Paterson, New Jersey shortly after James' death. It is uncertain as to Jane's date and place of death.

We cannot continue forward without describing some of the pending facts concerning our great grandmother Sophia's date and place of birth and death. The background of our great grandmother, Sophia Klein, has been difficult to establish with certainty. We have established a few possible links. For example, there is a New York Immigration and Passenger list showing a Sophia Klein arriving in New York, on March 11, 1846 at the age of 9, with her mother, also Sophia, age 33.[66] Their trip originated in Germany with a departure from London on the ship *Switzerland* arriving in New York with her three siblings, Caroline, age 11, Catharine, age six, and Wilhelmine, infant. This ancestral thread looks promising. Concomitantly, there is an 1865 New York census which lists a Sophia 'Kline', age 26, born in Germany, living with her parents Christian, age 56, and her mother, Sophia, age 52, Cohocton, Steuben, New York. Per the 1865 census, Sophia, her parents, and sister, Katrina, age 22, were all born in Germany. In contrast to these two possible links, the 1855 New York census and the 1870 United States census document that Sophia was born in New York the same as her husband James. Thus, for now, time and place of birth seems to be a bit conflicting. Further research is ongoing to determine New York or German origins for Sophia.

Most recently, however, further research has documented a more credible link to Sophia's background. A previous 'Wilmot' researcher brought to our attention that the individual with the first name 'Muriel' listed on the grave-holding, 4-13-D-15 "Wilmott", in Calvary Cemetery, might be Sophia. To substantiate this claim we inquired and received certified Certificate of Death, 129113, from the New York Department of Records and Information Services.[67] The certificate notes that a Muriel Wilmot, age 35, died from Phthisis Pulmonalis (tuberculosis or consumption)

---

[65] U. S. City Directories, 1822-1995. (2011). Patterson, New Jersey, City Directory. 1874. Digital Images. Ancestry.com.

[66] Sophia Klein. (2003). New York, Immigration and Passenger List, 1820-1850. Ship: *Switzerland*, Family Identification: 117678. Ancestry.com.

[67] Muriel Wilmot. Certificate of Death 129113. New York City Department of Records and Information Services, Municipal Archives.

and diarrhea, on September 7, 1872. Her birthplace was indicated as New York and she had been a resident of New York since birth. Both parents' birthplace was identified as Germany. The place of death was 30 Broome Street, Thirteenth Ward (Manhattan). Muriel Wilmot was buried at Calvary Cemetery on September 9, 1872. Interestingly, the death certificate indicates that she had endured this illness for sixteen months and three days having been attended by H.T. Topping, M.D. (Note: The certified copy of the death certificate shows that the first name which appears to be 'Muriel' was written over another first name which began with the first letter 'S'.) We then searched the New York Herald newspaper to see if we could find an obituary for Muriel. Ironically, we found an obituary in the September 8th, 1872, edition of the newspaper for a 'Maria Willmot'.[68] The obituary read as follows:

> "Willmot. – On Saturday, September 7, of consumption, Maria Willmot, wife of James Willmot, aged 35. The relatives and friends of the family are respectfully invited to attend the funeral from her late residence, 30 Broome Street, on Monday afternoon, at two o'clock, thence to Calvary Cemetery."

As a result of the findings of the certified Certificate of Death from New York City's Municipal Archives coupled with the corresponding obituary from The New York Herald, we have great confidence that 'Muriel', 'Maria' and Sophia are one and the same person. Accordingly, a follow-up certified search of the death records by the New York City Department of Records and Information Services for the Borough of Manhattan for the years 1870, 1871, and 1872, unfortunately found no listing for the name Sophia Wilmott/Wilmot.[69] This now makes sense since it appears the name on the Certificate of Death may have been changed from Sophia to Muriel and for what reason we do not know; however, it was not uncommon for names on either census or birth/death documents to be misconstrued or illegible. (*see* Certificate of Death below).

---

[68] Maria Willmot Obituary. (1872, September 08). The New York Herald, page 5. Digital Images. Library of Congress, Washington, D.C.
[69] Sophia Wilmott/Wilmot. New York City Department of Records and Information Services, Municipal Archives, 24 January 2018.

"All permits for the removal of the body of any deceased person from the City of New York for Interment, and all Burial Permits, and Permits for the Disinterment of the remains of deceased persons in the City of New York, shall be granted and signed by the Register of Records."

☞ The Physician who attended any person in a last Illness is responsible for the presentation of this Certificate, accurately filled out, to the BUREAU OF RECORDS OF VITAL STATISTICS, within 36 HOURS after said person's death.— [See Sec. 150 of Sanitary Code.]

No PERMIT FOR BURIAL WILL BE GRANTED WITHOUT A PROPER CERTIFICATE.

# CERTIFICATE OF DEATH. 129113

1. Full Name of the Deceased, ( Write legibly and spell correctly. If an infant not named, give parents' names. ) *Mystala Wilmot*  Color, *White*

2. Age, *55* years, months, days.

3. Single, Married, Widow or Widower, (Cross out the words not required in this line.)

4. Occupation,

5. Birthplace, *New York* (And how long in the United States, if of foreign birth.)

6. How long resident in this City, *Since birth*

7. Father's Birthplace, (The State or Country.) *Germany*

8. Mother's Birthplace, (The State or Country.) *Germany*

9. Place of Death, No. *36 Broome* Street, *13th* Ward.

10. Number of Families in House, living separately, *Sixteen*

11. **I Hereby Certify,** That I attended deceased from *August 15th 1871* to *Sept 7 1872* that I last saw *her* alive on the *6th* day of *Sept* 1872, that *She* died on the *7* day of *Sept* 1872, about *3* o'clock, A.M. or P.M., and that the Cause of *her* death was :

FIRST, *Phthisis Pulmonalis*

SECOND, (Remote or complicating.) *Diarrhoea*

All the above information should be furnished by the Physician.

Time from Attack till Death :
(Write opposite each cause—if unknown it should be so stated.)

*Sixteen months*
*3 days*

Place of Burial, *Calvary Cemetery*

Date of Burial, *Sep 9th 1872*

Undertaker, *John Grey*

Place of Business, *507 Grand St*

Signed by *H. F. Töpffing*, M.D.,

Medical Attendant, Address, *72 Lexington St*

Certificate of Death - Muriel or Sophia Wilmot - September 7, 1872

Grave-holding, 4-13-D-15, "Wilmott", located in Calvary Cemetery, New York

The grave-holding, 4-13-D-15 "Wilmott", in Calvary Cemetery, Woodside, Queens, New York, was purchased on April 30, 1862, by James Wilmott. There are 11 burials in this grave holding. The grave site was originally purchased for James and Sophia's son James who died after six months. In addition, the early burial of Charles Kline was for James' brother-in-law, Sophia's brother. No headstone existed until December 17, 2017, at which time the Wilmot family had a headstone placed at the gravesite in memory of all ten 'Wilmott's' and Charles Kline. See below for the relationship of those listed:

Charles Kline: age 26, 1862, Brother-in-law to James and Sophia's brother.
James: age 6 mos., 1862, son of James and Sophia.
Michael: age 57, 1867, great-great Grandfather.
John: age 4, 1870, 'unknown relationship'.
Mary: age 7 mos., 1870, 'unknown relationship'.
Muriel: age 35, 1872, possibly Sophia - great Grandmother.
James: age 43, 1874, great Grandfather.
Peter: age 3 days, 1874, son of James Wilmott and Jane McIntyre.
John J.: age 1, 1875, 'unknown relationship'.
Margaret: age 'missing', 1879, possibly William Wilmott's wife, James' sister-in-law, possible age, 43.
John Wilmott: age 61, 1901, James Wilmott's brother, great-uncle.

In tribute to the burial of our ancestors listed above, the following poem by an unknown author reflects our thoughts of those we can now know and cherish.


*Dear Ancestor(s)*

*Your tombstone stands among the rest; neglected and alone,*
*The name and date are chiseled out on polished marbled stone.*
*It reaches out to all who care, it is too late to mourn.*
*You did not know that I exist. You died and I was born.*
*Our blood contracts and beats a pulse entirely not our own.*
*Dear ancestor, the place you filled one hundred years ago*
*Spreads out among the ones you left,*
*who would have loved you so.*
*I wonder if you lived and loved. I wonder if you knew*
*that someday I would find this spot,*
*and come to visit you.*

Author Unknown

## Historic Note:

Between 1850 and 1870, New York City's population grew from 550,394 (1850); 813,669 (1860); to a total of 942,292 inhabitants in 1870. A growth rate of 71.2 percent in only twenty years. The State of New York's population in 1870 was 4,382,759.

During the 1870s, Ulysses S. Grant, Union Civil War General, was elected and served as president of the United States from 1869 -1877 at which time Rutherford B. Hayes was elected and served for one term (1877-1881). Both presidents served during the Reconstruction era, a period after the Civil War during which the United States faced challenges of reintegrating into the Union the states that had seceded and determining the legal status of African Americans. The Fifteenth Amendment to the US Constitution was ratified in 1870 which prohibited federal and state governments from denying a citizen the right to vote based on that citizen's race, color, or previous condition of servitude. The Panic of 1873 was a financial crisis that triggered an economic depression in the United States and Europe from 1873 to 1877. Major League baseball began in 1876 with the Chicago White Stockings being the first team. They represented the National League.

# JAMES A. WILMOT

## (Grandfather 1868 to 1941)

Between 1868 and 1873, James A. Wilmot(t), the son of James and Sophia and our grandfather, began his life in an environment of familial uncertainty. James A.'s actual birth date; however, is somewhat obscure with several conflicting documents placing his birth year between 1868 and 1873. The evidentiary documents include: death certificate which indicates a birth date of August 28, 1868; an 1870 U.S. census (taken in January 1870) indicates James A. as six months of age, which would approximate an August 1869 birth date; a letter from the Children's Aid Society which noted James A.'s birth date as August 28, 1870; and a U.S. World War I draft registration card dated September 12, 1918, which indicated James A.'s date of birth as August 18, 1873 (the World War I draft registration card birth date may have been exaggerated as a response to President Woodrow Wilson's extension of the draft age range from 18 to 36 years of age to 18 to 45 years of age. However, James A. subsequently did not serve in World War I).

Early life for James A. had to be filled with considerable hardship during the meager times and everchanging environment of Manhattan, New York. His mother, Sophia (our great grandmother), is assumed to have died September 7, 1872. James A. inherited a step-mother, Jane McIntyre, when Jane married James A.'s father October 20, 1872. Less than two years later, James A.'s father, James (our great grandfather), died in August of 1874. Interestingly, an 1874 U.S. City Directory lists a Jane Wilmott, a widow, husband James, living at 122 Maple Street, Paterson, New Jersey. If Jane had left Manhattan after James' death in 1874, then the supposition is that James A. had been left to live with relatives. This supposition was substantiated by a letter from the Archives Office of The Children's Aid Society, New York, addressed to Bob Wilmot (June 2, 2015), upon inquiry of information relating to James' (A.) previous upbringing in Manhattan, New York.[70] The letter noted that a Mr. Harris of the Home of the Friendless had verified that James Wilmot was "surrendered," March 23, 1878, to the Home of the Friendless by his Aunt, Mrs. Peter Wilmot of 76 Mangin Street, New York. Mrs. Peter Wilmot stated, "she had a large family of her own and was unable to keep him (Peter Wilmot was our great-grandfather James' brother). His father, also named James, and mother, Sophia, were both dead." The letter continues by stating that on June 4, 1878, James Wilmot came to the Children's Aid Society from the Home of the Friendless – "James was age 8 and born on August 28, 1870." Thus, from the time James A. was born until he landed in the care of the Children's Aid Society, he had endured an unsettled beginning amidst the impoverished neighborhoods of early Manhattan in the late nineteenth century.

---

[70] *See* Documents re: Children's Aid Society letter to Bob Wilmot, 2 June 2015, pages 125-126.

1880 'New York City Slum' depicted by cartoonist William Allen Rogers.
W.A. Rogers was an American political cartoonist for Harpers Weekly
and the New York Herald.

## Children's Aid Society – Orphan Train:

It is important to note, that in the late nineteenth century, more than 1.2 million poor people lived in crowded tenements in New York City and when these tenement buildings filled up, thousands of people had no choice but to live in the streets, beneath bridges or in open lots. The alleys and sidewalks of New York City were filled with throngs of children which the police referred to as "street arabs."[71] Some of the children were abandoned, some had run away from home and some were orphans. Thus, it was the initial aim of the Children's Aid Society, created by Charles Loring Brace in 1853, to get these children off the street and to provide food, lodging, and clothing to these homeless children as well as to provide educational and trade opportunities; however, overtime, the program became so large that they were unable to care for all of them. Brace then conceived the idea of the Orphan Train,[72] a movement as a means of taking children, mostly orphans, out of the poverty of the city and to transport them to rural America, hopefully for a better future. As time went on, over the next seventy years trainloads of children traveled to rural Midwest and beyond. Some estimates by researchers suggest that approximately 150,000 to 400,000 children were transported by orphan trains over the seventy-year span with an estimate of approximately 100,000 being placed in Missouri.[73] However, it must be noted that the concept of 'placing out' orphans via orphan trains was not solely confined to the Children's Aid Society during this time frame. Other groups such as Boston's Children's Mission, the New York Foundling Hospital, and the Philadelphia Women's Industrial Aid Association followed Brace's example.[74] During this time, it was not uncommon for families in which one or the other parent had died and the living parent found themselves unable to support the family and as a result, they would place a child or children in an orphanage. In James A.'s case, his aunt was in a similar position and found it best to surrender him to an orphanage.

Sometime between June 4, 1878, when James A. first arrived at the Children's Aid Society and March 1879, J.P. Brace (Charles Loring Brace's brother), an agent of the Children's Aid Society placed James A. with George W. Carson of Boonesboro, Howard County, Missouri, via the Orphan Train. Interestingly, Charles Loring Brace effectively used the cheap fares of nineteenth century railroads in his orphan train plan. For fifteen dollars, a ticket could be purchased to send an orphan from New York City to a new home in Missouri. "Cheap fares, the central location of the state, and numerous small farming towns along the railroad tracks made Missouri

---

[71] Patrick, D. and Trickel, E. G. (1997). Orphan Trains to Missouri. University of Missouri Press, Columbia and London.
[72] Patrick, D. and Trickel, E.G., p.6.
[73] Patrick, D. and Trickel, E.G., p.10.
[74] Holt, M. I. (1992). The Orphan Trains – Placing Out in America. University of Nebraska Press, Nebraska and London.

a hub for the orphan trains even though many areas of the state were still considered to be the 'Wild West'."[75]

## The 1880s

On June 5, 1880, the 1880 United States Federal Census for Boonslick, Howard County, Missouri, listed James Wilmot as living with G.W. Carson, age 37, and his wife Lanora, age 25. G.W. and Lanora had two daughters, Elley B., age 6, and Eliza C., age 3. G.W.'s occupation was noted as farmer. James, age 9, was listed as a border having been born in New York

By March 1881, Mr. Carson had written to Mr. Brace requesting that Mr. Brace place James in another home. It is uncertain if Mr. Brace placed James A. in another home; however, eight years later, on June 1, 1889, Mr. Carson wrote to the Children's Aid Society to inform them that James A. still lived in the area and was residing in Sisborn (Osborn?), Howard County, Missouri. Interestingly, on September 14, 1889, James had also written to the Children's Aid Society. "James wrote that Mr. Carson promised him a saddle, a bridle and a good suit of clothes if James stayed until he was 21. Mr. Carson was very hard on him and after 4 years James would not stay and moved to Mr. Hardin Maupin's home. Mr. Maupin [had] died and James remained with his son James Maupin." James further added "that he had not had many advantages and was working for $1.50/day on the river. The Children's Aid Society continued to track James A. and noted that between December 28, 1889, and April 19, 1890, James had a good home at a farm with W.D. Ainsworth, Boonesboro, Missouri. However, "James was very anxious to learn the whereabouts of his relatives." And finally, an inquiry was submitted on June 29, 1895, to the Children's Aid Society, that an attorney from Marshall, Missouri, had asked for information on James Wilmot; however, no mention of the attorney's name or why an attorney was seeking information on James. (*see* Documents: Children's Aid Society Letter, pages 125-126.)[76]

## Personal Note:

We should take a moment and comment on the trials and tribulations in which James A. had to endure during his adolescent years. Being separated from his siblings never to know their whereabouts or any of his extended family in New York had to be heartbreaking. As James A. noted, from the time he arrived at the Home of the Friendless March 23, 1978, up to his last reported residence with Mr. Ainsworth on April 19, 1890, at the age of 20, "he had not had many advantages." As we shall see, over time, his life would follow a similar disadvantaged path coupled with the burden of never knowing the whereabouts of his relatives.

---

[75] Patrick, D. and Trickel, E.G., p. 50.
[76] The Children's Aid Society Letter (*see* Documents).

## George W. Carson:

Howard County, Missouri was settled in the early 1800s after the Louisiana Purchase in 1803. Lewis and Clark had camped there in 1804 and 1806 on their expeditionary trip to and from the Northwest Passage and the Pacific Ocean. One of the early settlers to the Missouri River territory in 1810 was Lindsey Carson (1754-1818) and his wife Rebecca. The Carson's developed their farm from a large tract of land that had been part of the Spanish land grant bought by the sons of Daniel Boone, prior to the Louisiana Purchase. It became known as 'Boone's Lick' for the salt deposits that the Boone family successfully mined. The Carson's and Boone's were close family friends that worked, socialized, and intermarried with each other.[77] This area became part of Franklin Township, Howard County, Missouri. Lindsey and Rebecca Carson had ten children. Two of the male children were Sarshall Cooper Carson (1816-1864) and his brother Christopher Houston 'Kit' Carson (1809-1868). Sarshall Carson was the father of George Washington Carson (1842-1928) who is the 'George W. Carson' noted in the letter from the Children's Aid Society as the individual James A. was initially placed with via the Orphan Train in Boonesboro, Howard County, Missouri. Thus, George W. Carson was the nephew of Kit Carson. It would have been interesting to know if James A. had knowledge of Kit Carson during his time with the Carson family. Both Lindsey and Sarshall Carson were buried in Boons Lick Township, Howard County, Missouri. George Washington Carson was buried in the Boonesboro Christian Church Cemetery.[78]

## Historic Note 1890s:

Most of the records for the 1890 United States Federal Census were destroyed by fire in 1921. This included the entirety of the State of Missouri's federal census records for 1890. Thus, the letter and information from the Children's Aide Society is the main historical documentation for the 1880 to 1890 time-period. Currently, the ten years from 1890 to 1900, is void of any documentation for James A. although the search is ongoing.

## The 1900s – 1920s

On June 27, 1900, the Twelfth United States Federal Census was taken which included Boons Lick (Township), Howard County, Missouri. The census indicated that James 'Willmoth' was living with John F. Black, age 61, and his wife Margaret, age 56, at this time. John F.'s occupation was farmer. James' birthdate was listed as January 1870, age 30, born in New York as

---

[77] Sides, H. (2006). Blood and Thunder, An Epic of the American West. Doubleday Publishing, New York. p. 10.
[78] Union Historical Company. (1881). History of Howard and Cooper Counties, Missouri. (2004). Hearthstone Legacy Publications, Missouri. Pgs. 158-164. Retrieved from https://catalog.hathitrust.org/Record/008653337.

were both his parents. James' occupation was noted as farm laborer. He could read, write, and speak English according to the census.

On July 11, 1901, J. A. 'Willmot' of Fayette, Howard County, Missouri, and Effie Sartain (grandmother), of Fayette, Howard County, Missouri, filed with the Justice of the Peace for a marriage license. J. A. was listed as over twenty-one years of age and Effie was listed as under eighteen years of age. The judge of the county court, H. Duran, married J. A. and Effie on July 14, 1901, at his residence. The Certificate of Marriage was recorded on July 22, 1901. (Note: In June 1900, Effie was living with her mother America in Chariton Township, Glasgow, Missouri. Glasgow was approximately twelve to thirteen miles by road from Fayette, Missouri. According to the 1900 U.S. census, James A. was living in Boons Lick, Missouri, and therefore he would have been in close proximity to both Glasgow and Fayette and would not have had far to go to court Effie prior to marriage.)

J. A. 'Willmot' and Effie Sartain, Marriage License - Fayette - Howard County, Missouri

Prior to James' marriage to Effie, the 1900 United States Federal Census for Glasgow, Chariton Township, Howard County, Missouri, taken on June 20, 1900, for family number 240, dwelling 238, indicated that Effie Sartain, daughter of America (Todd) Sartain was age 16, born September 1883, in Missouri. The census further indicated that Effie was a student and could read, write, and speak English. According to the census Effie had a sister, Gracie age 13, born June 1886, and 'Zachie' (Zachariah), age 11 born November 1888. All three children were students at the time of the census. America Sartain was noted as head of household, age 38, born October 1861, and divorced. The census shows America's occupation as 'farmer' and it further recorded that she owned her own farm (although mortgaged). Ironically, the next family listed on the census, family number 241, was Matthew Sartain, head of household, age 42, born April 1858, and divorced. America and Matthew were still living in the same proximity. (Matthew 'C.' was Effie, Gracie, and Zachie's father, America's previous husband and our great grandfather.) Matthew was also a farmer like America, however, he owned his own farm clear of any mortgage. (Note: Further review of the 1900 United States Census shows Granville Sartain, age 70, and his wife Rebecca, age 55, living at a farm nearby as family 232, dwelling 232. Granville and Rebecca, Matthew's parents, are our great-great grandparents. Further observation of the 1900 federal census shows a multitude of Sartain relatives living on farms in the Chariton/Fayette area. Although of interest, for now, the Sartain thread will be developed later under its own historical/genealogical lineage.)

America (left) - Effie (top) - Zachie (middle) - Gracie (bottom) - Matthew C. (right)

Circa late 1890s

49

Between 1902 and 1906, James A. and Effie had three children, all boys. Orville Price Wilmot, May 26, 1902; Noble King Wilmot (father), August 3, 1903; and William Howard Wilmot, January 14, 1906. All were born in Fayette, Howard County, Missouri. Effie is assumed to have died sometime after William's birth although date and place of burial are uncertain. At this time no other records have been found regarding our grandmother Effie. (Note: The Sartain family had their own cemetery in Howard County, Missouri, and it is uncertain if Effie may have been buried there. The first indication of Effie's middle name, Alice, was indicated on Noble King Wilmot's death certificate. Noble King did maintain correspondence with Effie's sister, our great aunt, Gracie Sartain Todd or 'Aunt Grace,' up through the 1960's.)

As of 1910, the United States Federal Census has been an elusive source for locating James A.; however, the census does show all three boys living with their grandmother (our great grandmother), America P. Sartain, in Cuervo, Guadalupe, New Mexico. *See* photo below with all three boys, America, and her daughter Grace Dell Todd.

At this time, we will take a brief departure from the Wilmot chronology and explain the brief New Mexico episode of America P. Sartain during the 1910 era.[79] On April 20, 1910, the thirteenth census of the United States for New Mexico, Guadalupe County, Cuervo Precinct, Number 6, identified America 'C.' Sartain, female, white, head of household, 48 years of age, and widowed. In addition, the census reported that America had had three children only one of which was living. America was born in Missouri as was her father (Peter Todd); however, her mother (Almira Anderson) was born in Kentucky. The census further stated that America could speak English, read, write, and was self-employed as a general farmer having owned her own farm free and clear. (Note: The farm consisted of 160 acres acquired by way of a land patent application obtained via the 1862 Homestead Act. At the time New Mexico was still a Territory and officially became a state in 1912.) Residing with America were her three grandsons: Orville P. 'Wilmott', male, age 7; 'Novle' Wilmott, male, age 6; and William H., male, age 4. The census further indicates that all three boys had been born in Missouri as was their mother (Effie Sartain); however, their father (James A.), was born in New York. Orville and Noble had attended school; however, it is uncertain whether it was Missouri or New Mexico. Interestingly, according to the census, living next to America was her daughter, Grace D. Todd, age 23, and her husband 'Clarance' E. Todd, head of household, age 28. Grace and Clarence had been married for two years having had one child who was no longer living at the time of the census. Like America P., Grace and Clarence were general farmers who owned their own farm most likely having filed for a land patent as well. (Note: The census states that America P. had given birth to three children (Gracie, Effie, and Zachariah), although only one of her children were living. If Grace was still alive, then this would indicate that Effie (our grandmother) had passed-away sometime between when William H. was

---

[79] America P. Sartain will be explored in more detail in a following series, *The Sartain Story*.

born in 1906 and a time prior to 1910 when America P. came to New Mexico with her three grandsons. Zachie must have died during this time frame as well.)

In addition to the 1910 census, the *Cuervo Clipper*,[80] the regional newspaper for Cuervo, Guadalupe County, New Mexico, referenced America P. Sartain or Mrs. Sartain in several newspaper publications. The newspaper column, 'Local Items,' noted in the December 2, 1910, edition, that "Mrs. Sartain has moved to Santa Rosa and is running the Ellison Hotel."[81] (Note: To date, no further information is available regarding the Ellison Hotel in Santa Rosa.) Another edition of the Cuervo newspaper dated, August 1, 1912, stated, "Mesdames Sartain, Monson and Hanson and her two little girls, were pleasant callers at the Clipper office Tuesday. Mrs. Sartain made arrangements to make proof on her homestead."[82] (Note: Please reference below, 'Historic Note: 1862 Homestead Act' regarding: the "proving up" requirements to obtain a land patent.) A few months later another edition of the newspaper referenced 'Mrs. America Sartain' on Thursday, October 24, 1912, which stated, "Mrs. America Sartain and her three grandchildren left last Thursday for their former home in Mo."[83] (*See* below the newspaper clipping). It would have been interesting to know the experiences the three boys would have had in New Mexico and the adventures America P. and Gracie had during these years in the Cuervo and Santa Rosa areas of New Mexico.

## Historic Note: 1862 Homestead Act

The Homestead Act of 1862 has been called one of the most important pieces of Legislation in the history of the United States. Signed into law in 1862 by Abraham Lincoln after the secession of southern states, this Act turned over vast amounts of the public domain to private citizens. Two hundred seventy (270) million acres, or 10% of the area of the United States was claimed and settled under this act. A homesteader had only to be the head of a household or at least 21 years of age to claim a 160-acre parcel of land. Settlers from all walks of life including newly arrived immigrants, farmers without land of their own from the East, single women and formerly enslaved people worked to meet the challenge of "proving up" and keeping this "free land". Each homesteader had to live on the land, build a home, make improvements and farm for 5 years (reduced to 3 years in 1912) before they were eligible to "prove up". A total filing fee of $18 was the only money required but sacrifice and hard work exacted a different price from the hopeful settlers. With application and receipt in hand, the homesteader then returned to the land to begin the process of building a home and farming the land, both requirements for "proving up" at the end of

[80] Cuervo Clipper. The University of New Mexico Digital Repository included issues published between 1/7/1910 through 12/1/1922. https://digitalrepository.unm.edu/cuervo_clipper_news/.
[81] Keeter, C. (1910). The Cuervo Clipper, 12-02-1910. https://digitalrepository.unm.edu/cuervo_clipper_news/44.
[82] Keeter, C. (1912) The Cuervo Clipper, 08-01-1912. https://digitalrepository.unm.edu/cuervo_clipper_news/88.
[83] Keeter, C. (1912) The Cuervo Clipper, 10-24-1912. https://digitalrepository.unm.edu/cuervo_clipper_news/96.

five years. When all requirements had been completed and the homesteader was ready to take legal possession, the homesteader found two neighbors or friends willing to vouch for the truth of his or her statements about the land's improvements and sign the "proof" document. After successful completion of this final form and payment of a $6 fee, the homesteader received the patent for the land, signed with the name of the current President of the United States. This paper was often proudly displayed on a cabin wall and represented the culmination of hard work and determination.[84]

Cuervo Clipper - October 24, 1912 - "Local Items"[1]

[84] National Park Service. (2019). Homestead Act.
https://www.nps.gov/home/learn/historyculture/abouthomesteadactlaw.htm.

Photo above: left to right: America P., William, Orville, Noble, Grace 'Gracie' Cuervo, Guadalupe, New Mexico, circa: 1910.[85]

---

[85] Cuervo, Guadalupe, New Mexico, today is located near Interstate Highway 40, approximately halfway between Amarillo, Texas, and Albuquerque, New Mexico.

# Historic Note: Fayette, Missouri, Birthplace of Noble, Orville, and William

Fayette, Missouri was established in 1823 and named after Gilbert du Motier, Marquis de Lafayette. Its population in 1900 was 2,717 as compared to an estimated population in 2016 of 2,695. The US population in 1900 was 76, 212, 168, a 21 percent increase over the 1890 United States Census. Missouri's population in 1900 was 3,106,665. Republican William McKinley was elected president in 1896 and re-elected in 1900. McKinley was assassinated in 1901 and Theodore Roosevelt, who was vice-president followed. The Spanish-American War (1898) was over. Henry Ford started the Ford Motor Company in 1903 and the World Fair in St. Louis began in 1904.

On September 12, 1918, at the Local Board for County Saline, State of Missouri, James A. Wilmot, from Grand Pass, Saline, Missouri, registered for the World War I draft, Serial Number 1381, Order Number A-514. James indicated his birth as August 18, 1873, age 45. James' occupation was listed as 'day laborer' with the Missouri Pacific Railroad. The registration noted James as being of medium height, medium build, light brown eyes, and brown/gray hair. *See* below. (Note: James did not participate in World War I.)

James A. Wilmot World War I Draft Registration - September 12, 1918

## The 1920s

The 1920 United States Federal Census found James A. 'Willmont' living in Waverly, Middleton Township, Lafayette County, Missouri, on January 8, 1920. James A. was listed as head of household, widowed, and 46 years of age. His birthplace was listed as New York as was his mother and father. At the time of the census he was working for a wage as a 'track laborer' for the railroad. The census noted he spoke English as well. Living with James A. were his three sons, Orville, age 17, Noble, age 16, and William, age 13, all were born in Missouri. None of the boys were listed as employed. (Note: In September 1918, James A. was working for the Missouri Pacific Railroad (MoPac RR) as a 'day laborer' according to his draft registration. Thus, it is likely that his occupation as 'track laborer' in the 1920 census was with the MoPac RR as well. The MoPac RR was the main railroad through Grand Pass and Waverly, Missouri, during this period. Interestingly, James A.'s son, Orville Price, also worked for the MoPac RR and eventually retired with a Railroad Retirement Pension in the mid-1960s.)

The above two photos of what appears to be railroad 'track laborers'
were saved by Noble K. Although uncertain, we believe that James A.
is possibly the person on the far left in the top photo and third from the right
in the bottom photo. To date, we have no positively identified photos
of our grandfather, James A.

## Historic Note – Waverly, Missouri:

From 1920 until his death, James A. Wilmot spent most of his recorded life in and around Waverly, Middleton Township, Lafayette County, Missouri. Waverly was a town on the Missouri River in the northern part of Middleton Township. Approximately, as early as 1845 a person by the name of W.W. Schroyer laid out a town in the western part of Waverly and called it Middleton. Its geographical location may have suggested the name: the town was on the Santa Fe Trail about halfway between Lexington and Marshall, the county seat of Saline County. The name is mentioned in 1867 as Middletown. In regard to the town and name of Waverly, Mr. J.W. Motte, a resident, writes, "As it was found inconvenient to have two small towns with an imaginary line between them, the citizens united to have them made one. Elisa M. Edwards, who was one of the committee to frame a charter and write the first by-laws for the united town and also to select a name, told me that a tailor working for him at the time told him that he had once lived in a little town in Illinois named Waverly, that it was a nice town and he liked the name. From a multitude of names suggested, Waverly was finally selected. Sir Walter Scott's novels probably influenced the decision as they were very popular at this time."[86] (Note: At the time Waverly was named, 'The Waverley' novels were a popular series of novels written by Sir Walter Scott between 1814 and 1832). In 1920 the population of Waverly was 810 and as of July 1, 2019, the population was 843.

## The 1930s

In 1930, the Fourteenth Census of the United States for Middleton Township, Lafayette County, Missouri, taken April 9, 1930, lists a James A. 'Willmot', age 56, born in New York, who owned and lived on a farm. Both his parents were listed as being born in New York. The census noted that James' was employed as a farmer engaged in general farming. Most interesting though, the census also states that James was married to Lotta 'Willmot', age 55, born in Indiana. Both Lotta's parents were also born in Indiana. So, it is somewhat uncertain if this is our grandfather, James A. Wilmot. Some of the factors which may show legitimacy is that James A. lived in Waverly, Middleton Township, Lafayette County, Missouri, during the 1920, 1930, and 1940 censuses. Waverly, Missouri's population peaked in 1930 at a total of 941, so there is not a huge population base with which to draw from with the Wilmot surname (with variations) plus, James A. had no family in Missouri having arrived on the Orphan Train when he was eight years old. Therefore, the Wilmot or Willmot surname would have been limited during this time in Waverly, Missouri. And, of course James A.'s age and date of birth has always been a precarious item throughout his life (although his age was documented as 46 in the 1920 census). That leaves the

---

[86] Atchison, A. (1937). Place Names of Five West Central Counties of Missouri. M.A. thesis., University of Missouri-Columbia.

oddity so to speak of Lotta 'Willmot'. The question is, who was she? A wife or a friend? There is no indication of James A. having been married to anyone other than Effie Alice Sartain. (Note: There is a reference to a Lottie Wilmot who married a John Duff, 1934, Waverly, Lafayette, Missouri. This would have made her 59 or 60 at marriage if it were the same person).

## **Historic Note:**

The 1930's in Missouri reflected much of midwestern United States' way of life which was greatly influenced by the Great Depression, the Dust Bowl, and high unemployment with difficult living conditions, especially for the small farmer. Herbert Hoover and Franklin D. Roosevelt were president during this difficult time. Other highlights included Jessie Owens' four gold medals at the 1936 Olympics and the crash of the German passenger ship, LZ 129 Hindenburg, at the Lakehurst Naval Air Station in New Jersey. Baseball greats such as Babe Ruth, Joe DiMaggio, Lou Gehrig, Ted Williams, Dizzy Dean, Lefty Grove, and Carl Hubbell helped lift the spirits during the Great Depression era.

On or about 1932 through 1940, James A. Wilmot (Willmott) had lived on a farm[87] consisting of 13.13 acres in Lafayette County, Missouri.[88] During this eight-year period, as per recorded Trust Deeds, this property had transferred from James A. to Orville and Bee 'Willmot' and back to James A. with Noble K. Wilmot having an initial promissory note interest as second party to the recorded Deed of Trust given to the Home Savings and Loan Association of Norborne, Missouri (first party). O.P. Willmot and Bee Willmot, his wife, completed their transfer of the Warranty Deed back to James A. on December 28, 1936. There were at least six Trust Deed's involving the Wilmot family regarding James A.'s farm up to January 21, 1937. On September 6, 1938, William H. Wilmot (son) purchased five and one-half (5 ½) acres more or less, adjacent to James A.'s farm. Compounded by the Great Depression, it was possible during this difficult time in the Midwest, that James A. was having trouble making payment on his 13.13 acres farm including the property taxes. Thus, on September 8, 1938, William H. entered into an agreement with James A. whereby William H. gave James A., 'the right to use and occupy' three-fourths (3/4) of an acre of William's five and one-half acres, 'as and for a home, for and during his natural life and free of any rent.' It was noted that Lexington County, Missouri, state and county property tax receipts for 1938 and 1939 show James A. as property owner of the 13.13 acres; however, 1940

---

[87] James A. Willmot's farm was identified via 1932 Lafayette County, Missouri, per state and county property tax receipts. However, it is unknown, at this time, the actual date of purchase.

[88] Legal description as of September 5, 1934: All of that part of the Northeast Quarter (1/4) of the Northwest Quarter (1/4) of Section Thirteen (13), Township Fifty-one (51), Range Twenty-four (24), being and lying south of the county or public road as it now runs through the above described land, save and except the right of way of the Missouri Pacific Railroad Company over and through the said above described land, the above described tract of land conveyed, together with the said right of way of the Missouri Pacific Railway Company, containing 13.13 acres more or less. All being and lying in the County of Lafayette and State of Missouri.

tax receipts show Wm. H. Wilmot as property owner of 18.63 acres which would have included James A.'s 13.13 acres plus the adjoining 5.5 acres that William H. had purchased in 1938. Therefore, William H. had assumed title to James A.'s farm sometime between 1938 and 1939. Unfortunately, William Howard Wilmot died on November 29, 1939. On November 26, 1939, William H. had filed his last will and testament declaring Noble K. Wilmot as executor of the will. The will provided nothing for either his father James A. or his brother Orville P. After all debts were paid, Noble K. was to receive all remaining real and personal property of William H. As required, Noble K. filed the last will and testament with the Saline County Probate Court on January 4, 1940. It was officially recorded with the probate court on January 8, 1940. The above noted property: the 13.13 acres was assessed at $250.00; and the 5.5 acres at $100.00. (Note: Noble K. paid the annual property taxes up to 1946 at which time the property was sold on April 16, 1946, for $450.00 to James O. Ritchart and Florence E. Ritchart of Saline County, Missouri. During the period after William H. passed-away, up until 1946, it is uncertain of the status of the farm, i.e., rented, farmed, etc. Per census data, James A. moved from the farm sometime in mid-to-late 1940 to the County Home in Lexington, Lafayette County, Missouri, where he died January 20, 1941.)

## The 1940s

The 1940 United States Federal Census, taken April 2, 1940, by the Bureau of Commerce, for Waverly, Middleton Township, Lafayette County, Missouri, shows a James 'L.' Wilmot, head of household living on a farm which was being rented. The census indicated James was widowed, age 76 and born in New York. Although James was listed as living on a farm the census further noted that he was not working and he was not seeking work; however, the census stated he had income from other sources. Also living with James on the farm were two lodgers: Luther Carey, widowed, age 78, born in Missouri; the other was W.M. Carey, single, age 40, born in Oklahoma. Luther was a fisherman and W.M. was a farmer. All three according to the census lived at the same location in 1935. None of them had attended school.

Not long after the 1940 census taken in April of 1940, James A. Wilmot passed away on January 20, 1941, 3:00 p.m., at the County Home, Lexington Township, Lafayette County, Missouri.[89] James A. died from chronic myocarditis (inflammation of the heart muscle) and edema of the lungs (excess fluid in the lungs). At time of death, he was 72 years, 5 months, and 2 days old with a birth date listed as August 18, 1868. He was born in New York City, New York. James A. had been a farmer and was widowed having been married to Effie Alice 'Sartan' Wilmot (her date and place of death/burial is uncertain). James A.'s parents' names and parents' place of birth were listed as 'unknown'. His son, Noble K. Wilmot, Omaha, Nebraska, was the informant. The funeral director was Harry Hershberger from Marshall, Missouri, and the subsequent burial took

---

[89] James A. Wilmot. Missouri State Board of Health, Bureau of Vital Statistics. Certificate of Death 11164.

place in Grand Pass, Missouri, January 22, 1941 (it is uncertain which cemetery). (Note: Per James A.'s certificate of death, there was only a reference to his place of birth, that being New York. Interestingly, James A.'s parents' names and place of birth were listed as 'unknown', thus indicating that his son, Noble K. Wilmot, the 'informant' at the time of death, had no apparent knowledge of either of his grandparents, James Wilmot and Sophia Kline Wilmot).

James A. Wilmot - Death Certificate - Missouri - 11164

Before we move on from our grandfather, James A., we must elaborate on his sister, Alice, and brother, William H., neither of which ended up in an orphanage nor on the Orphan Train. First, in 1870, James' sister, Alice (or Alles), our great-Aunt, was 11 years old as indicated in both 1870 U.S. censuses (already discussed above.) The obscure 1860 U.S. census (also discussed above) stated that Alice was eleven months old in July 1860 when the census was taken. This would indicate that Alice was born in approximately August of 1859 and approximately ten years older than James A. Records indicate that Alice 'Willmot' married Henry Schilling on September 20, 1877. At this time, there are no records of Alice's death or burial; however, Henry died at the age of 37, July 27, 1894, in Ogden, Utah. Henry's brother, Adam, had the body brought to Cheyenne, Wyoming, for burial a few days later. It is unknown if Alice lived or died in Ogden, Utah, she would have been approximately 33 years old at the time of Henry's death.

Next, James A.'s brother William H. (possibly Henry) Wilmot was born between 1862 and 1867 based on varied U.S. censuses. He was approximately two years older than James A. He married Clara M. Pfau prior to 1900 (based on the 1900 U.S. Census) and they had a daughter Emily (Emelia). According to the New York Death Index, William H. Wilmot died on June 18, 1933, in Bronx, New York, at age 66. Clara died on February 26, 1943, Bronx, New York, at the age of 73 according to the New York Death Index. Their daughter, Emily Clara Wilmot Winter, died on October 22, 1991, in New York (possibly the Bronx) at the age of 91.

## Historic Note - 1940s:

The biggest impact of the 1940s was World War II, the "War Years" 1941-1945, and the atomic bomb. The Nuremburg Trials followed and the creation of the United Nations. Franklin D. Roosevelt died in his fourth term in office and vice-president Harry S. Truman took the helm subsequently besting Thomas E. Dewey in the following 1948 presidential election. Winston Churchill became Prime Minister. Jackie Robinson joined the Brooklyn Dodgers. China became communist and George Orwell's "Ninety Eighty-Four" was published. Of course, by the end of the decade the U.S. was pulled into another conflict - the Korean War which commenced in June 1950.

# NOBLE KING WILMOT

## (Father) (1903-1984)

Noble King Wilmot was born August 3, 1903, in Fayette, Howard County, Missouri, to James A. and Effie Alice Sartain Wilmot(t). The 1910 United States Census taken April 20, 1910, for Cuervo Precinct, Guadalupe County, New Mexico, lists 'Novle' K. Wilmot, male, age 6, living with his widowed grandmother, America 'C.' Sartain, age 48, as family unit 48. Currently, it is unknown what the status of his parents were during the 1910 national census. According to the census, America was a farmer and head of household who owned her own farm, spoke English as her native tongue, and could read and write. She was born in Missouri as was her father (Peter Todd), and her mother (Almira Anderson) was born in Kentucky. Also living at the Sartain household was Noble's brothers, Orville P., male, age 7, and William H., age 4. Both Noble and Orville were attending school at the time. The census noted that the boys' father was born in New York and their mother was born in Missouri. Living next door as family unit 49 was America's daughter (Noble's aunt), Grace D. (Grace Dell) Todd, age 23, and her husband, 'Clarance' E. (Clarence Edward) Todd, age 28, both having been born in Missouri. At the time of the census they had been married for two years having had one child who was no longer living. Both Grace and Clarance spoke English as their native tongue and could read and write. Clarance Todd was a farmer and they owned their own farm as well. (Note: Reference the earlier photo located on page 53, which shows the three boys with America and Grace in Cuervo, Guadalupe County, New Mexico.)

The 1920 U.S. Federal Census taken January 8, 1920, for the 2nd Ward of Waverly Town, Middleton Township, Lafayette County, Missouri, found Noble 'Willmont,' age 16, living with his widowed father, James A., age 46, and his two brothers, Orville, age 17, and William, age 13. The family lived in a rented dwelling and James A. provided a living as a truck laborer for the railroad. All three boys were unemployed although they were all attending school and all three could speak English, read, and write. The census indicated that James A. could neither read nor write. The three boys were all born in Missouri and James A. was born in New York as was his mother (Sophie?) and father. The boys' mother (Effie Alice) was born in Missouri according to the census. (Assumption: Noble King is an uncommon given name and middle name. My assumption is that because Noble was born in August his name derives from the meaning of the word august. August can mean Noble and/or Kingly which in turn, lends itself to the name Noble King Wilmot. I remember when I was young, our dad mentioned to me that being noble was a synonym of august….I didn't believe him but I looked it up and indeed it did….it took me a long time to put it together).

Noble (bottom right) - Circa Early 1920's

Noble - Circa Late 1920's or Early 1930s - 1<sup>st</sup> row, 3<sup>rd</sup> from right
Noble was an avid baseball player in and around Grand Pass and Missouri City.

The post-World War I era of the 1920s[90] saw Noble K. enter Grand Pass High School, Grand Pass, Saline County, Missouri, in September of 1920, at the age of 16.[91] Noble previously attended Saline County Public Schools, District of Grand Pass, Missouri, where he completed the 8<sup>th</sup> grade on May 9, 1919. Courses he took in high school included arithmetic, algebra, geometry, English composition, English literature, economics, American history, American government, and

---

[90] Note: World War I lasted from July 28, 1914, through November 11, 1918. A male Citizen could sign up for military duty at the age of 18; however, Noble and Orville were too young to enter the war and William was handicapped. The organized draft did not start until the Selective Service Act of 1917 which initially targeted male citizens between the ages of 21 to 35. The draft ages changed over time during the war.

[91] Grand Pass is a village in Saline County, Missouri. Grand Pass was named from the Osage Pass that passed through the town. In 1930 the population was 168 and in 2010 the population was 66.

physical geography. Noble graduated from Grand Pass High School on May 15, 1924, at the age of 20. A total of four students were in the 1920 graduating class which included Noble and three others: Armin Henry Bueker, Morrison D. Fenner, and Floyd Benny Wehmeyer. Most interesting is the class motto: "The Elevator to Success is Not Running - Take the Stairs." *See* below the copies of his report cards, final high school record, and Commencement Exercises at the Methodist Church in Grand Pass.

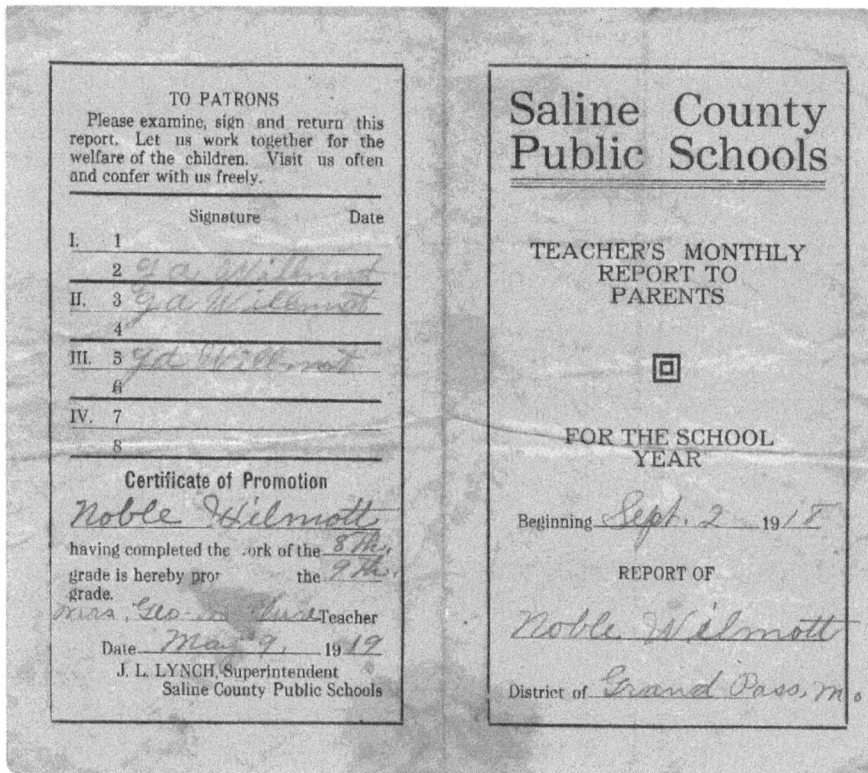

Promotion from 8th grade to 9th grade - Saline County Public Schools
Grand Pass, Missouri

GRAND PASS CONSOLIDATED SCHOOLS

Pupil's Report Card    192_3_192_

PUPIL _Noble Wilmot_    Class _IV_

_Jas. O. Huston_    PRINCIPAL

| | 1st Quar. | 2d Quar. | 3d. Quar. | 4th Quar. | Average |
|---|---|---|---|---|---|
| Days Absent | 3½ | 1 | 6 | 5 | |
| Times Tardy | 0 | 0 | 0 | 0 | |
| Neatness | G | G | G | P | |
| Conduct | S | S | S | E | |
| Effort | S | S | S | S | |
| English | G | S+ | G | G | G |
| History | | | | | |
| Mathematics | G | S | | | |
| Agriculture | | | | | |
| Hygiene | G | G | S– | S– | G+ |
| Science | | | | | |
| Civics | | | | | |
| American Gov't | | | | | |
| Economics | S– | G+ | | | |
| Soc. | | | G | S– | S+ |
| Book Keeping | | | S | S | S |

Promoted to _Graduation_ Grade  _G. Alan Markland_ Teacher.

High School Graduation - Grand Pass Consolidated Schools

Grand Pass High School, Grand Pass, Mo.

PERMANENT-FINAL HIGH SCHOOL RECORD

Name _Wilmot, Noble K._    Course
Parent or Guardian _Wilmot J. A._    Residence _Grand Pass, Mo._
Entered from _Grade school_    Date Entered _Sept 1921_    Age at Entrance _16_

Standing at School Last Attended

| SUBJECT | 1st Year | | | 2nd Year | | | 3rd Year | | | 4th Year | | | 5th Year | | | SUBJECT | 1st Year | | | 2nd Year | | | 3rd Year | | | 4th Year | | | 5th Year | | |
|---|---|---|---|---|---|---|---|---|---|---|---|---|---|---|---|---|---|---|---|---|---|---|---|---|---|---|---|---|---|---|
| | 1st | 2nd | Cr. | 1st | 2nd | Cr. | 1st | 2nd | Cr. | 1st | 2nd | Cr. | 1st | 2nd | Cr. | | 1st | 2nd | Cr. | 1st | 2nd | Cr. | 1st | 2nd | Cr. | 1st | 2nd | Cr. | 1st | 2nd | Cr. |
| English Comp. | G | G | 1 | G | G | 1 | | | | | | | | | | Credits For'd | | | | | | | | | | | | | | | |
| English Lit. | | | | | | | E | E | 1 | | | | | | | Arithmetic | | | | | | | | | | S | G | | | | |
| Home Econ. | | | | | | | | | | | | | | | | Plane Geometry | | | | G | G | 1 | | | | | | | | | |
| Latin | | | | | | | | | | | | | | | | Solid Geometry | | | | | | | | | | | | | | | |
| Sociology | | | | | | | E | E | | | | | | | | Adv. Algebra | | | | | | | S | ½ | | | | | | | |
| Agriculture | G | G | 1 | | | | | | | | | | | | | Bookkeeping | | | | | | | | | | S | ½ | | | | |
| Physical Geog. | | | | G | | ½ | | | | | | | | | | Commercial Law | | | | | | | | | | | | | | | |
| Com. Geog. | | | | G | | ½ | | | | | | | | | | Stenography | | | | | | | | | | | | | | | |
| French | | | | | | | | | | | | | | | | Typewriting | | | | | | | | | | | | | | | |
| Ancient History | G | S | 1 | | | | | | | | | | | | | Economics | | | | | | | G | ½ | | G | ½ | | | | |
| Amer. History | | | | | | | S | E | 1 | | | | | | | Manual Training | | | | | | | | | | | | | | | |
| M. & M. History | | | | G | S | 1 | | | | | | | | | | Mech. Drawing | | | | | | | | | | | | | | | |
| Civics | | | | | | | | | | | | | | | | Dom. Science | | | | | | | | | | | | | | | |
| Ele. Science | | | | | | | | | | | | | | | | F. H. Drawing | | | | | | | | | | | | | | | |
| Botany | | | | | | | | | | | | | | | | Music | | | | | | | | | | | | | | | |
| Physics | | | | | | | | | | | | | | | | Physical Ed. | | | | | | | | | | | | | | | |
| Chemistry | | | | | | | | | | | | | | | | Am. Lit. | | | | | | | S | E | 1 | | | | | | |
| Physiology | | | | | | | | | | | | | | | | Mo. Hist. | | | | | | | G | | ½ | | | | | | |
| Algebra | G | G | 1 | | | | S+ | | ½ | | | | | | | Am. Govt | | | | | | | G | ½ | | | | | | | |
| Credits For'd | | | 4 | | | 3 | | | 1½ | | | | | | | Total Credits | | | | | | | | | 1 | | 2½ | | 1½ | | |

Graduated _May 1924_    Standing    Dropped    Course

Number units accepted from other schools (Indicate on record with red ink).    _G. Alan Markland._
_Supt of Schools._

Permanent - Final High School Record, Grand Pass, Missouri

# *Commencement Exercises*

—of—

## GRAND PASS HIGH SCHOOL

### METHODIST CHURCH

### THURSDAY EVENING, MAY 15, 1924

Song—"America" _____ Audience

Invocation _____ Rev. B. F. Wharton

Piano Solo _____ Geraldine Simmons

Address of Welcome _____ Floyd Wehmeyer

Music _____ Orchestra

Farewell Address _____ Armin Bueker

Piano Trio
    Elizabeth Jones, Lorena Bueker, Edris Zeysing

Address to Graduates _____ Hon. Edgar A. Shook

Music _____ Orchestra

Presentation of Diplomas
    C. A. Jones, Sec'y. Board of Education

Benediction _____ Rev. Wharton

---

### CLASS ROLL

Armin Henry Bueker      Morrison D. Fenner
Floyd Benny Wehmeyer      Noble King Wilmot

### CLASS COLORS
Old Rose and Silver

### CLASS FLOWER
Pink Rose

### CLASS MOTTO
The Elevator to Success is Not Running
Stairs
the
Take

Commencement - Noble King Wilmot - Grand Pass

A month after graduation from high school Noble prepared to attend the War Department of the United States', Citizens' Military Training Camp (C.M.T.C.), Seventh Corps Area, Fort Leavenworth, Kansas. Noble's first step was to find a doctor. Regulations stipulated that prior to training, first-year men had to undergo a preliminary physical examination by a physician, the results of which were recorded and submitted along with verification of inoculations for smallpox and typhoid fever several months before reporting to camp (see vaccination certificates below).[92] In Noble's case, his noted physician was Earl H. Coon, a local resident M.D. from Grand Pass and a Captain (Medical Officer) with the Officer Reserve Corps (ORC). (Note: The War Department's C.M.T.C. Headquarters for the 7th Corps Area was Omaha, Nebraska). After the physical in June, Noble proceeded to travel to and attend the C.M.T.C. at Fort Leavenworth, Kansas, from August 1, 1924 to August 30, 1924. Upon completion of the course, Noble's Military Training Certificate verified that he had completed the Basic Course, Infantry Branch, at the Fort Leavenworth camp. According to Noble's certificate, courses completed at the camp included physical training, citizenship, drill, marksmanship: rifle; and, hygiene, sanitation and first aid. (Note: The Military Training Certificate states, that "only young men in good physical condition were accepted for attendance at Citizens' Military Training Camps.") Upon completion of the basic course, he was recommended by H. B. Wheeler, Executive Officer, to the Camp Commander, Brigadier General Harry A. Smith, to continue his training by attending the advanced "Red" course during the following summer of 1925 (see Military Training Certificate below). Over the subsequent holidays the commanding officers, Brigadier General Harry A. Smith and Major General George B. Duncan extended greetings to the 1924 C.M.T.C. graduates with the "hopes [that] you will return next year (1925) to help build the best C.M.T.C. in the world," (see below the Holiday and Christmas greetings).

Noble's trip to Fort Leavenworth, Kansas, was probably his first big trip out of state. A few letters he retained from this period were most interesting. His anxiousness of being away from home for the first time was clearly evident in several letters he had sent back home. One was received as early as August 3rd, three days after he arrived at camp. Earl H. Coon, M.D., Grand Pass, MO, was one individual he felt comfortable writing to. Dr. Coon's letters addressed to "Friend Noble" were filled with local news and encouragement for Noble's new environment. Noble probably took solace with Dr. Coon's advice since Dr. Coon was not only his administering physician from Grand Pass, but he was familiar with military training as an active Captain with the Office Reserve Corps. Dr. Coon told Noble that, "maybe things are not just what you supposed it would be but by the time you are in a week or ten days, things will smooth out and run along O.K." "By this time, you ought to know what it is [like] to meet up with some real fellows." Dr. Coon had read in the local paper that there was to be a "gymkhana" (a day event of athletic competitions) and conveyed to Noble that, "you ought to shine in some of those events." Typical

---

[92] Kington, D. M. (1995) Forgotten Summers: The Story of the Citizens' Military Training Camps 1921-1940. Two Decades Publishing; San Francisco, California. page 59.

of small towns, Dr. Coon found an interested audience at the local post office where he would read out loud a letter from Noble for all to hear. Dr. Coon wrote that, "everyone was interested and some of them acted sort of foolish – I guess you get the idea of what I mean." (Perhaps Noble had a few admirers!) Other correspondence was with a friend or girl friend named Margaret from Grand Pass (last name unknown) which expressed typical feelings of young people separated for a first time. I am sure Noble felt proud upon graduation along with his recommended promotion to the "Red" course for the next summer (Note: We have no record that Noble attended the Red course the following summer.)

(Personal observation: Our dad was extremely interested in Boy Scouts both for his sons and for other boys entering scouting after his sons had moved on. One wonders if the regimentation learned at the C.M.T.C. was the seed for his desire to lead and teach the fundamentals of scouting. *See* the section on Boy Scouts.)

Tear along dotted line
**WAR DEPARTMENT**                    No. ...........

Certificate of Vaccination
against Typhoid and Paratyphoid Fevers
For Attendance at a Military Training Camp

I CERTIFY that *Noble King Willmot*
(Name. Write plainly)

whose address is _____ *Grand Pass      Mo*
(No. Street or R.D. No.)   (City)      (State)

was given typhoid-paratypnoid prophylaxis by me on

(date) *June 20 192*  (date) *June 27 1924* and completed
First dose                Second dose

on (date) *July 2   1924*
Third dose

*Earle H Coon M.D.*
Physicians signature. Sign both copies
*Capt. med. O.R.C.*
*Grand Pass   Mo*
address

Applicant will hold this
copy and deliver it to
the commanding officer
upon arrival at the
training camp.

---

Tear along dotted line
**WAR DEPARTMENT**                    No. ...........

Certificate of Vaccination
against smallpox
For Attendance at a Military Training Camp

I CERTIFY that *Noble King Willmot*
(Name. Write plainly)

whose address is _____ *Grand Pass   Mo*
(No. Street or R.D. No.)   (City)   (State)

was vaccinated against smallpox by me on *June 27  1924*
(date)

and that the result was   successful - unsuccessful.
Srike out word not applicable

Applicant will hold this
copy and deliver it to
the commanding officer
upon arrival at the
training camp.

*Earle H Coon M.D.*
Physicians signature. Sign both copies
*Capt. med. O.R.C.*
*Grand Pass, Mo.*
address

War Department Vaccination Certificates
for Citizen's Military Training Camps

# MILITARY TRAINING CERTIFICATE.

## Citizens' Military Training Camps

TO ALL WHO SHALL SEE THESE PRESENTS, GREETING:

KNOW YE, THAT *Noble King Wilmott*

HAS ATTENDED THE *Basic* COURSE OF INSTRUCTION.

*Infantry* BRANCH, AT THE CITIZENS' MILITARY TRAINING

CAMP HELD UNDER THE AUSPICES OF THE WAR DEPARTMENT OF THE UNITED STATES

AT *Leavenworth, Kansas*

FROM *Aug 1st* TO *Aug 30th* ONE THOUSAND

NINE HUNDRED AND TWENTY-FOUR

GIVEN AT *Leavenworth* THIS *30th*

DAY OF *August* IN THE YEAR OF OUR LORD ONE THOUSAND

NINE HUNDRED AND TWENTY-FOUR

REMARKS: *Discharged per Par. 11, S.O. 63 Hqs 7th*
*Leavenworth Kansas dated 8/30/24*

*[signature]*

*Brigadier General*

COMMANDING

W. D., A. G. O. Form No. 124
April 15, 1924
3—8139

Citizens' Military Training Camp - Military Training Certificate, Front Page

72

# CERTIFICATE OF TRAINING

Keep this Certificate.
It is valuable as a personal record and is evidence of your
Military Training.
Present it whenever you seek employment.
In case you join any of the Military forces of the United
States show it to each Commanding Officer who may be
placed over you.

I hereby certify that the candidate whose name appears on this certificate has been given training and instruction in the following subjects in the _____ *Basic* _____ Course, _____ *Infantry* _____ Branch, at this camp:

(Strike out the words not applicable.)

1. Physical Training.
2. Citizenship.
3. Hygiene, Sanitation, and First Aid.
4. Drill.
5. Marksmanship: Rifle and Pistol.
6. Combat Principles or Tactics.
7. Topography and Orientation.
8. Duties of Officers and Noncommissioned Officers.
9. Gunner and Cannoneer.
10. Equitation and Horsemanship.
11. Care of Animals, Material, and Hippology.
12. Motor Transport.
13. Driving and Draft.
14. Field Work and Service Practice.
15. Reconnaissance and Signal Communication.
16. Field Gunnery, Firing Data, and Conduct of Fire.
17. Coast Artillery.
18. Field Fortification and Demolitions.
19. Roads, Bridges, and Rigging.
20. Duties of Engineers.

The above-named candidate has completed the _____ *Basic* _____ Course, _____ *Infantry* _____ Branch, at this camp. He is recommended * _____ *to attend training in Red course* _____

He has been † _____ as a _____ in the _____ Branch

_____
(Component and organization, if any.)

Remarks ‡ _____ *Cost / hat.* _____

For The Camp Commander

*H. B. Wheeler* , Commanding.

Executive Officer

* Show recommendations in accordance with Par. 17, AR 350-2200.
† Indicate if candidate has been enlisted, examined for appointment, or appointed in any component of the Army of the United States while at camp.
‡ If candidate is under 21 years of age, indicate if certificate of qualification has been granted. Show property loss if any.
NOTE.—Only young men in good physical condition are accepted for attendance at Citizens' Military Training Camps.    3—8130

GOVERNMENT PRINTING OFFICE

Citizens' Military Training Camp - Military Training Certificate
Back Page

Brigadier General Harry A. Smith

sends

Christmas Greetings

to you and to all the students of the

Fort Leavenworth Citizens Military Training
Camp, 1924

and hopes you will return next year to
help build the best C. M. T. C. in the world.

Major General George B. Duncan

sends

Holiday Greetings

to you and to all students
of the
Seventh Corps Area
Citizen's Military Training Camps
and hopes you will attend the
1925 Camps

Holiday and Christmas Greetings - Seventh Corps Area and
Fort Leavenworth Citizens Military Training Camp Graduates - 1924

## Historic Note – C.M.T.C:

The authority for conducting the C.M.T.C. was the National Defense Act of 1920, signed into law by President Woodrow Wilson on June 4, 1920. The actual seed for establishing the training program for young civilians was planted by General Leonard Wood, Chief of Staff. It was Wood's political and public-relations savvy that launched the training program as an attempt at military preparedness. The volunteer C.M.T.C. program endured a twenty-year stint from 1921 to 1940. The age in which to qualify for selection to the summer camps run by the U.S. Army, was from 16 years of age to 30 years of age, with the highest numbers selected between the ages of 17 and 19. Applications in 1924 for the C.M.T.C. camps numbered about 50,000 from which 32,000 were selected for training at 28 summer camps, an increase of about 8,000 from the year before. (Note: the 28 camps were spread from coast to coast with one in Puerto Rico. By 1930 the number of camps swelled to 53 with 38,000 participants). The recruits provided their own transportation to the camps, some by car, some by train, some hopping boxcars, and some by government transportation. Uniforms were provided. An individual, if promoted each year, could be selected to attend the following year's four-week summer course. The courses were identified as: Basic, Red, White, and Blue courses. Over time, six Army branches of service were offered: Infantry, Cavalry, Field Artillery, Coast Artillery, Corps of Engineers, and Signal Corps. The programs were geared to increasingly advance more sophisticated military training and leadership throughout the collective programs. A few recruits upon completion of the Blue course were promoted to Lieutenant. The courses included daily military instruction, ceremonies, physical training, range practice, and study time for the advanced courses. Athletic games were provided which instilled competition for medals in sports such as swimming, track, boxing, tennis, and baseball (non-military skills). The weekends were free time. Unfortunately, by 1941, with World War II looming for the United States, the C.T.M.C. camps were suspended due to the "vitally important and immediate task of training combatant forces." Essentially, the days of the C.T.M.C. were over.[93]

From the time Noble completed the C.T.M.C. training in August 1924 until June of 1926, we are uncertain of his background, employment, etc. However, from June 1926 to November 1926, he documents himself on several employment applications as working for O.E. Peters, Missouri City, Missouri, with an annual salary of $1,000.00. His place of employment was Grand Pass, Missouri, and he worked as a clerk on a road construction job keeping time, making purchases, etc. Following his brief stint with O.E. Peters, Noble gained further employment with

---

[93] Kington, D. M.

the Massman Construction Company, Kansas City, Missouri, starting in April of 1927. His immediate supervisor was F. Pitts and his duties were described as clerk and timekeeper of construction work although it was also noted that Noble did occasional construction work as well. He was based out of Grand Pass, Missouri, with an annual salary of $2,400.00. Noble relinquished his position with Massman Construction in May of 1929 at such time as being hired by the federal government with the War Department, U.S. Engineers, Kansas City, Missouri. (Note: Noble grew up along the Missouri River not only working but hunting and fishing. His two years with Massman Construction obviously laid the groundwork for his lifelong work with the U.S. Army Corps of Engineers and the Missouri River.)

## Historic Note – Massman Construction Company:

Massman Construction Company originated in 1908 under Harry J. Massman and continues in operation today as a family owned business specializing in heavy civil and marine construction. Massman's first contract was for the Missouri Pacific Railroad installing rip rap along the riverbanks to protect the railroad tracks near the small town of Napoleon, Missouri. Other riverbank projects ensued and within a few years the firm had expanded its fleet of floating equipment. Massman was working on river bank stabilization projects along the entire length of the Missouri River, as well as a wide variety of work for railroads and other private enterprises. In the mid-twenties when Congress authorized the creation of a 6-foot deep channel in the Missouri River from its mouth to Omaha, Nebraska, Massman was able to apply its expertise and floating equipment toward the successful completion of several large contracts with the Corps of Engineers.[94] (Note: Most interesting is the fact that, as teenagers, our dad found us similar employment with construction companies that were working various projects along the Missouri River. His position as an Army Corps of Engineers Inspector for Missouri River projects provided ample contacts. Keith, for example, worked three summers, '67, '68, and '69, as a laborer at the Fort Calhoun Stone Company, a rock quarry adjacent to the Missouri River in Fort Calhoun, Nebraska. This facility quarried rip rap to be either trucked or moved by barge to stabilization projects, i.e., dikes, along the Missouri River. Bob also worked with construction companies such as Cunningham-Kiewit Construction Company and Pentzein, Inc. both from Omaha, Nebraska, which contracted for marine/river projects on the Missouri River in the late 1960's. Note: Also during the1960s, Noble's other son James started work with the U.S. Army Corps of Engineers as a draftsman in the Omaha, Nebraska office).

Noble had transitioned from his employment with the Massman Construction Company to the War Department, U.S. Engineers, Kansas City, Missouri, in May of 1929. He was employed

---

[94] Massman Construction Company. (2020). History. Retrieved from https://www.massman.net/history.

as a Chief Inspector of contract work supervising and inspecting accomplished work. His immediate supervisor was F.Y. Parker, Area Engineer, and his annual salary was a respectful $1,800.00 (the average annual salary in the U.S. in 1930 was $1,368.00). He continued in this position through August of 1930. During this time, Noble had met a young lady by the name of Mary Louise Crabtree. It followed that on May 17, 1930, Noble K. Wilmot, age 26, of Grand Pass, Saline County, Missouri, and Louise Crabtree, age 25, of Missouri City, Clay County, applied for marriage in Clay County, Missouri (Marriage Application License 15794). The application was recorded by Nicholas Mosby, Recorder of Deeds for Clay County, Missouri. Noble and Louise were subsequently married the same day, May 17, 1930, in Liberty, Missouri.

Mom and Dad

Interestingly, the 1930 U.S. Federal Census taken on April 24, 1930, for Missouri City, Fishing River Township, Clay County, Missouri, shows Louise living with her parents, James A. (James Allen), age 58 (grandfather), and Mami (Anna Mary 'Mamie' Foley Crabtree), age 56 (grandmother), along with a sister, Evelyn, age 12, and a brother J.A., age 17. She was not employed at the time according to the census. This was but a few weeks prior to Louise and Noble getting married. In contrast, the current search for Noble K. for the 1930 U.S. Federal Census has resulted in negative results (same as with Noble K.'s father, James A.).

Although we have yet to find 1930 census information, we have found residential information for 1931 and 1933. According to the 1931 Kansas City, Missouri, City Directory, Noble K. Wilmot was living at 515 Maple Blvd, Apt. 34. Two years later, in 1933, the City Directory for Kansas City, Missouri, identifies Noble K. Wilmot and M. Louise Wilmot living at 521 Maple Blvd., Apt. 21. Noble K.'s occupation was listed as Inspector.[95]

In 1933, while living in Kansas City, Missouri, Noble joined the Masonic Lodge. Specifically, Rural Lodge No. 316, A.F. & A.M. (Ancient Free and Accepted Masons). This lodge is the fourth oldest in Kansas City having been organized in March of 1869.[96] Noble was 'initiated' into Freemasonry, first in the degree of Entered Apprentice, on September 18, 1933. On November 6, 1933, he was 'passed' to the degree of Fellowcraft and finally, on December 8, 1933, he was 'raised' to the degree of Master Mason.[97] (On April 1, 1958, Noble's lodge membership was transferred to the Omaha Centennial Lodge, Lodge 326, where he remained as a member until his death in 1984).

---

[95] U. S. City Directories, 1822-1995. (2011). Kansas City, Missouri, City Directory. 1931, 1933. Digital Images. Ancestry.com.

[96] Union Historical Company. (1881). The History of Jackson County, Missouri, containing A History of the County, Its Cities, Towns, etc. Birdsall, Williams and Co., Kansas City, MO. Retrieved from https://catalog.hathitrust.org/Record/008653337.

[97] Noble K. Wilmot's Masonic information was taken from his Masonic Member Profile, Nebraska A.F. & A.M. provided by Robert K. Wilmot, also a Master Mason.

The above photo is a 2019 photo of apartments 511, 515 and 521 Maple Blvd., Kansas City, Missouri, 64124 (Maple Terrace). The (3) three-story buildings were built in 1917.

From August 1930 through August of 1935, Noble remained at the U.S. Engineers office in Kansas City, Missouri. Per his job application, his title and duties were noted as Inspector - in charge of checking and maintaining all field construction reports and writing the monthly and annual report for the Area Office. In addition, he assisted in the preparation of the annual report to the Chief of Engineers, Washington, D.C. His annual salary was $2,100.00. From August 1935 to April 1936, Noble remained with the U.S. Engineers but he was transferred to the Maintenance Section making the monthly stock inventory for the Kansas City District and preparing the report for the District Engineer. In addition, he made the monthly inspection of stone quarries in the Kansas City District. On April 12, 1936, he was transferred to the Omaha District Office, Omaha, Nebraska.

We move on to the year 1937 in which a church publication, the 'Beau Knot News',[98] in Kansas City, Missouri, described the early days of Noble and Louise's relationship as follows:

"Several years ago, a winsome lass named Louise Crabtree was drinking a coke in a drug store at Missouri City, Mo. Into the pill place walked her future husband-Noble Wilmot. Having nothing at the present time to do, they struck up a conversation and found they had a lot in common.

Being in Government service, Noble immediately was transferred to a nearby town. However, he went back to Missouri City every Sunday to play ball. Naturally, the baseball game didn't last all day and so Noble had time to call on Louise. Before long, they fell in love and Noble said Louise finally got him. They were married May 17, 1930 in Liberty, MO, and moved to Kansas City where they have spent most of their time since."

(Note: On July 8, 1932, Noble and Louise had their first child, a girl, Mary Lu. They would have been living in Kansas City at the Maple Blvd. Apartments at the time – reference above photo).

"Dainty little Mary Lu is, of course, the pride and joy of the Wilmot family. She is going on five years of age although she looks younger because of her size.

Louise has lived in Missouri City most of her life. She was graduated from both ward and high schools and was very active in the Missouri City Christian Church.

Noble was born in Grand Pass, Missouri. After he was graduated from high school he [also] attended Missouri Valley College at Marshall, Missouri. He took his civil service examination in 1929 and is now an inspector in the War Department, U.S. Engineers. He is quite an all-around sportsman – playing, basketball, baseball, and tennis.

Louise is quite domestic – she likes to cook, sew, keep house – although Noble tells us that she plays a corking game of tennis.

The Wilmot's were so in hopes that they would be able to stay in Kansas City, but the Government has transferred Noble to Omaha. They are certainly fine examples of a Christian family and we hate to lose them. We Beau-Knots wish for them the best of everything in their new home and want them to know that we will always be anxious to hear from them at any time. We hope that it won't be long before Noble will be able to get

---

[98] Beau Knot News, 1937, Edition 1, Volume 7, Lamonte Roach, President, and Dr. J.T. Ferguson, Teacher. Kansas City, Missouri. We are not sure which Christian church in Kansas City, MO.

located in Kansas City permanently – because its people like the Wilmot's that make our class what it is."[99]

Unfortunately, nine months after Noble and Louise had moved to Omaha, on January 5, 1937, Noble was furloughed without pay. Correspondence from Noble for re-employment stated that, "Due to a reduction in force on account of lack of work in the Omaha District, I was furloughed without pay effective the close of business, January 5, 1937." In the midst of the Great Depression this probably came as a shock; however, Noble was certainly aware of the uncertainty of employment since he was originally transferred to Omaha due to a fifty percent reduction in force at the Kansas City District Office. Noble must have made good personnel contacts because by January 8, 1937, he had received notice from B.J. Hayes, Personnel Clerk, of an opening for an 'Engineer's Aide' in the Procurement Section at the Omaha District Office with an annual salary of $1,800. Noble applied and received an offer for the position from Captain L.W. Prentiss, Corps of Engineers, on January 21, 1937, with a start date of February 1, 1937. Noble accepted the position probably with great relief. From February 1, 1937 to July 23, 1940, Noble had moved to the Construction Section at the Omaha District Office under his supervisor, E. H. Toman. His annual salary increased over this time-period to $2,3000. His job duties were similar to his earlier positions which included preparing and writing reports but more specifically for the Division Engineers where he wrote reports relating to construction projects and labor data. One item of interest is that Noble, during his early years in Omaha, 1938-1939, took a one-year extension course at the Municipal University, Omaha, Nebraska, completing three semester hours in Engineering Drawing and three semester hours of College Algebra. Later, Noble received commendations for participation in relief efforts during the Missouri River floods of 1943 and 1952 in and around Omaha. After the historic floods, he became an inspector with the Flood Protection Division with the Omaha District Corps of Engineers. (*See* newspaper article below).[100] Noble remained employed with the U.S. Army Corps of Engineers, Omaha District Office, retiring as a Civil Engineer of Construction in 1969 after forty and a half years of service, May 1929 – November 1969. (Note: Noble's early job descriptions were taken from job application forms and correspondence during his early career.)

---

[99] Beau Knot News.
[100] Council Bluffs Nonpareil (Council Bluffs, Iowa). (1956). Online Publication. Digital Images. Ancestry.com (2006). Retrieved from https://www.ancestry.com/interactive/8290/NEWS-IA-CO_BL_IO_NO.1956_03_06_0017/501323793?backurl=https%3a%2f%2fwww.ancestry.com%2ffamily-tree%2fperson%2ftree%2f81211940%2fperson%2f260046611370%2ffacts&ssrc=&backlabel=Return.

contend a quorum was lacking.

The new rector, chosen by the vestry, was installed by the Rt. Rev. James P. DeWolfe, bishop of Long Island.

The Rev. Mr. Melish did not attend the ceremony in the 102-year-old church on Brooklyn Heights.

### Three Months Old, Tiny Baby Boy Now Strapping 5-Pounder

WHITTIER, Calif. ℗ — A boy who weighed 1½ pounds when he was born last Nov. 30 goes home from the hospital Tuesday, a strapping 5 pounder.

The family physician says the youngster, Steven Lee Danielson, is doing fine. He is the third child of Mr. and Mrs. John Danielson of nearby Rivera. Mrs. Danielson

chines for cultivating, harvesting and other operations.

## Army Engineers Inspect Levees

The Omaha District Corps of Engineers Tuesday was making its semi-annual inspection of the Council Bluffs levee system.

The inspection was being carried out by Noble K. Wilmot of the flood protection division. He was accompanied by employes of the Public Works Department and Eldon Evans, of the Evans Construction Co. here.

The Evans firm has been awarded the 1956 contract for maintaining the 15 miles of levee along the Missouri River and Indian Creek.

## Historic Note:

The early 1930s was a happy time and a time of good fortune for Noble and Louise being newly married and being employed. However, for the country in general, this was a time in which the Roaring Twenties had declined and the Great Depression, following the stock market crash in 1929, was gathering traction at an unprecedented rate under newly elected President Herbert Hoover. (Note: It took until 1954 for the Dow to fully recover from the 1929 crash). The depression continued under newly elected Franklin Delano Roosevelt in 1933. Unemployment climbed to 24.9 percent which led to initiatives such as the Civilian Conservation Corps and the Civil Works Administration to help boost employment. Extreme heat and dust bowls added to drought conditions which in turn had a further deterrent effect on the economy. Conditions worsened until the late 1930s when at such time, a return to normal had slowly begun. This was a time when being employed was a godsend. Unfortunately, good times were stymied when Japan attacked Pearl Harbor on December 7, 1941, and as a result, Congress declared war on Japan and subsequently the United States' entry into World War II.

## The 1940s

The 1940 U.S. Federal Census, taken on April 8, 1940, for Omaha, Douglas County, Nebraska, found Noble K. Wilmot, age 36, Louise, age 35, and Mary 'Lou', age 7, all living together at 4516 Poppleton Street. Their residence was rented for $50.00 per month. The census indicated that Noble had completed four years of high school, Louise had completed one year of high school, and Mary Lou had finished the first grade of elementary school. All three were born in Missouri and previously, in 1935, they had all lived in Jackson County, Missouri. At the time, according to the census, Noble was working as a Clerk in the Engineering Department, United States War Department, for an annual wage of $1,920.00. (Note: The City Directories for Omaha, Nebraska, in both 1938 and 1940, also listed Noble K. and M. Louise Wilmot as living at 4516 Poppleton. Noble's occupation was noted as Inspector, U.S. Engineers).[101]

The year 1941 started on a sad note. On January 20, 1941, Noble's father (our grandfather), James A. Wilmot, passed-away at the County Home, Lexington Township, Lafayette County, Missouri. He was buried at Grand Pass, Missouri (cemetery currently unknown). However, by July 26, 1941 things brightened for Noble and Louise. They welcomed their second child into the family, a son, James Noble Wilmot. By this time, Noble and Louise had moved a few blocks away to 4540 William Street, according to the 1942 City Directory for Omaha. Mary Lu at the time was attending Beals Elementary School, 1720 South 48th Street.

---

[101] U. S. City Directories, 1822-1995. (2011). Omaha, Nebraska, City Directory. 1938, 1940. Digital Images. Ancestry.com.

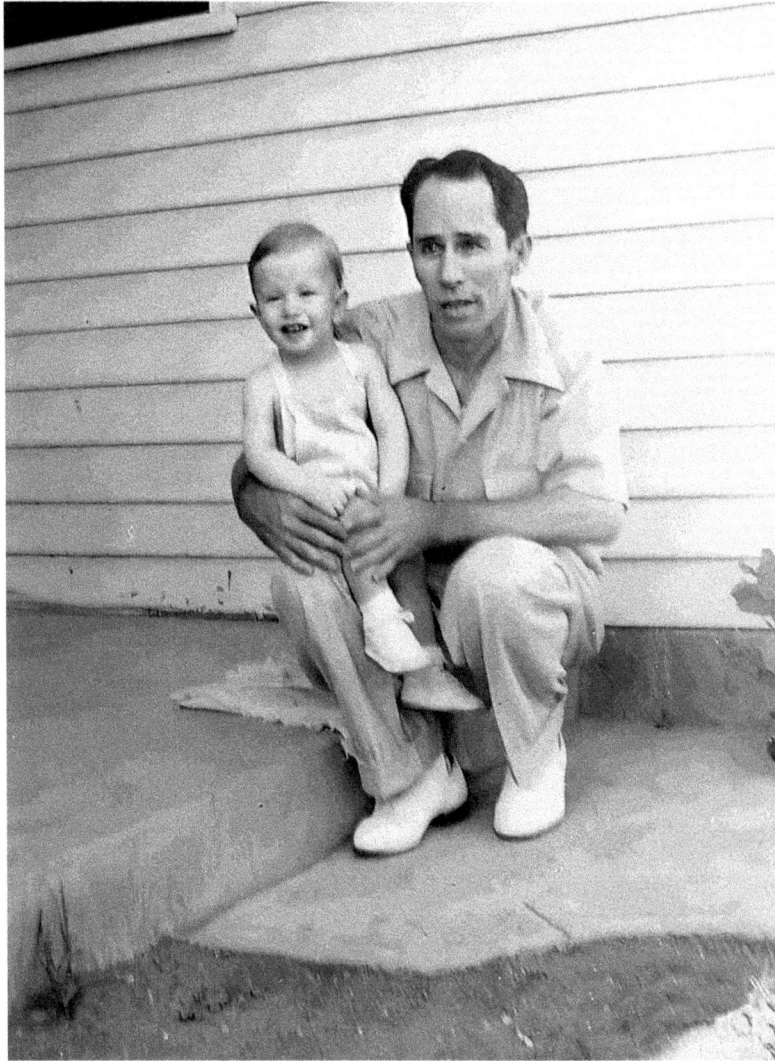

Jim and Dad - 1942

On February 14, 1942, the U.S. World War II draft card index identifies Noble King Wilmot as registering for the draft in Omaha, Douglas County, Nebraska, at the age of 38.[102] The draft index indicates Noble was employed with the U.S. Engineers, War Department. His physical description was described as 5'6", 135 lbs., ruddy complexion, brown eyes, and black hair (*See below*). (Note: Noble was not called up to active duty).

Noble King Wilmot - World War II - Registration Card

[102] U.S. World War II Draft Cards Young Men 1940-1947. Digital Images. Ancestry.com. (2011).

1302 South 51$^{st}$ Avenue, Omaha, NE (as of June 2020)

Sometime in early 1942, the Wilmot family moved into a new residence. The house was located on a corner at 1302 South 51$^{st}$ Avenue, or 51$^{st}$ Avenue and Poppleton Street. At the time, this was newly developed residential housing. (Noble would reside here until the mid-1970's when he moved a few blocks north to 801 So. 52$^{nd}$ Street, the Masonic Manor.) Shortly after Noble and Louise took up residence in their new home, two more were added to their family. A second son, Robert King was born November 20, 1944, and the third son, Keith Alan born July 20, 1947.

## Church:

      We are not exactly sure which Christian church Noble and Louise attended while in Kansas City, Missouri (reference Beau Knot News above); however, we do know that upon their move to Omaha in the early 1940s, Noble and Louise did join the First Christian Church (Disciples of Christ) located at the corner of 26th and Harney Street in Omaha (see photo below) where they attended both Sunday School and Church Services each Sunday. Noble held many positions in the church from Deacon to Elder and from Chairman of the Board of Deacons to Chairman of the Board of Elders. He was also the Membership Chairman from 1951 to 1952. Noble was an active member helping the minister with Boy Scouts and their God and Country Awards, contributing to youth sports, e.g., softball and basketball, and donating to regular various church pledges. Louise was active with the Church Choir and the weekly social and volunteer women's groups. All three boys were baptized in the church. Sunday was a special day for the Wilmot's and one thing for sure, Noble and Louise made sure their three boys were in church every Sunday and in turn, made sure they attended youth group each Sunday night (perfect attendance was important). In addition to Boy Scout camps in the summer, Noble and Louise made sure the three boys all attended Church summer camps as well. Sometime in the early 1960s, the First Christian Church at 26th and Harney Street was torn down and a new church built at 66th and Dodge Street. Noble and Louise were founding members of the new church and were faithful and active members up to the time of their passing.

First Christian Church - 26th & Harney Street, Circa 1950s

## Continuing Census Information:

The 1950 U.S. Federal Census and the subsequent census years which follow are not available due to the "72-Year Rule". According to the "72-Year Rule," the National Archives releases census records to the public, 72 years after Census Day. As a result, the 1930 census records were released April 1, 2002, and the 1940 records were released April 2, 2012. The 1950 census records will be released in April 2022.

## Scouting:

In September 1951, Noble began his volunteer service to the Cub Scouts and Boy Scouts of America in Omaha. Initially, he was an avid parent and Pack Committee Member (Cub Scouts) for Troop 97 as a means in which to introduce his son, Jim, to the scouting environment. Interestingly, our mother, was a Den Mother for the Cub Scouts participating until all three sons had advanced to Boy Scouts. Noble, advanced to Troop Committee Member (Boy Scouts) for Troop 97, MESCA District, in February 1953 (probably Jim's first year in Boy Scouts) and advanced to Scoutmaster in February 1960 serving in this capacity through September 1964. Noble also helped organize an Explorer Post (advanced Boy Scout program) for Post 97 and Post 327 during this same time-period. As Scoutmaster, he was a 'master' at organizing camping trips for Troop 97 during all seasons of the year usually culminating with the weeklong summer camp at Camp Cedars near Cedar Bluffs and Fremont, Nebraska. During his tenure as advancement chairman and Scoutmaster with Troop 97, there were 33 scouts receiving the Eagle Award, 3 receiving the Silver Explorer Award, 6 receiving the God and Country Award and 7 receiving one or more of the palms (silver, bronze and gold). (During this period, 1953-1964, throughout the nation, less that 2 percent of all Boy Scouts received the Eagle Scout award each year). Noble's three sons all received the Eagle Scout and God and Country Scout awards with Jim achieving the Silver Explorer award. All four, Noble and his three sons were members of the Order of the Arrow Ordeal. Noble received the Special Merit Award from the MESCA District, Covered Wagon Council for Outstanding Service and Leadership as Scoutmaster of Troop 97, Boy Scouts of America, in August 1963. After 1964, Noble served in many capacities such as merit badge councilor, neighborhood committee member, and leadership training. He received the Twenty-Year Service Award for his dedication to scouting in September 1971.

Through scouting, Noble, as a dad, was a great role model for his sons and as a special award for each of them, he sent each on a unique summer scouting trip: Jim to a Boy Scout Jamboree at Valley Forge (1956); Bob to Philmont Scout Ranch in New Mexico (1958); and, Keith to a Boy Scout Jamboree in Colorado Springs (1960). Moreover, Noble's volunteer efforts did not stop with scouting, he was also a Charter Member of the Boys Club of Omaha and an avid supporter of the Omaha Home for Boys both through leadership and financial donations. So, in addition to scouting, one can certainly say that our dad was vigilant in trying to help not only his own three sons get started on the right foot in life, but other less fortunate 'kids' as well. (Note: Interestingly, our dad had noted in his documented 'Personnel Record' that early on, "I was a Boy Scout with seven other boys in a newly organized Boy Scout Troop in a country church in 1916. The troop did not function a year and I am not sure it was chartered. I did not have further access to Boy Scouting." Noble's brief experience with scouting had followed the early founding of the Boy Scouts of America in 1910, by William D. Boyce.)

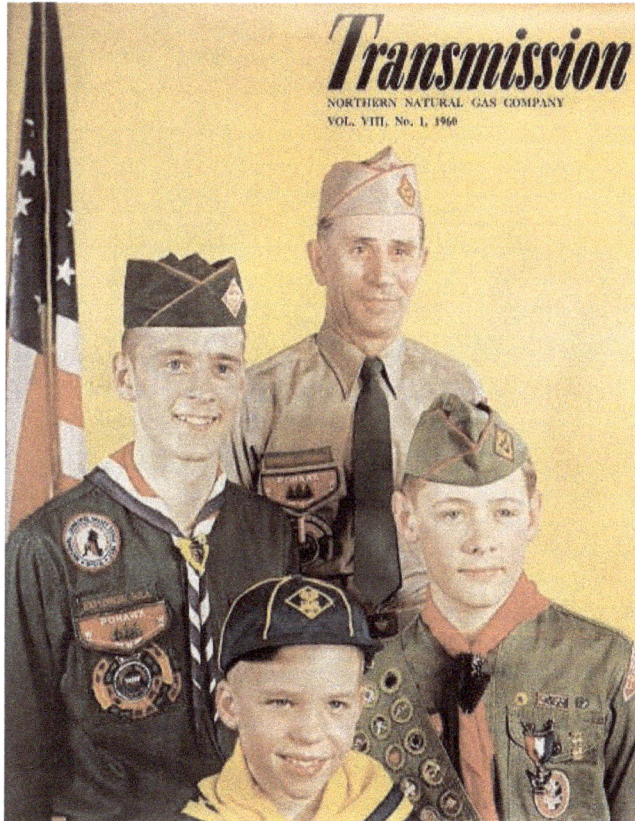

The above photo was on the cover of the Northern Natural Gas', National Magazine, *Transmission*, 1960, as a tribute to the Boy Scouts of America's 50-year anniversary of scouting, 1910-1960. Noble was selected as the Scoutmaster for the photo along with the Explore Scout, Boy Scout and Cub Scout, all of which represented the Covered Wagon Council, No. 326.

## Hunting and Fishing:

Noble was an avid hunter and fisherman in his early days; however, his time afield was somewhat limited once he married and his family grew. After his mother passed-away, he and his brothers would hunt and fish to help make ends meets. Being raised along the Missouri River allowed for ample opportunity. Noble always said he had to make each shot count because ammunition was expensive. His favorite instruction was to always shoot a rabbit in the head in order to save the meat. From experience, he could even do this while the rabbit was running; however, there was the time when he shot the rabbit running past the car (1950 Mercury) and did not realize the car was behind the rabbit. A shotgun has many pellets, many of which decorated the side of the car. A lot of ribbing came with this hunting trip. Of interest, I have posted below copies of some of his hunting licenses. I, and sometimes Bob, were along on many of the hunts which would take us to Wayne, Nebraska, for pheasants and quail (sometimes a rabbit or two, maybe a jack rabbit too), to Missouri Valley, Iowa, for ducks (Jim Eagleton's lease), to the Forney Lake, Iowa, area for ducks (he even hunted this area prior to the 1952 flood), and also to farms in southern Nebraska for pheasants and quail. We compared experiences with the Forney Lake, Iowa, area because when he hunted ducks there the Missouri River was still untamed and when I hunted there 35 years later, it was a State controlled goose hunting reserve (although you could still hunt ducks). He would always shoot his Savage automatic 12-gauge shotgun which would inherently jam, but then that just added to the bantering from fellow hunters such as Jim and Frank Strnad, 'Cooney' Cognard, Walt Seaman, and Rudy Larsen. All were a hoot to be around on hunting excursions. Family fishing was not really the best experience with the Wilmot family; however, Noble tried and had taken the family fishing to Lake Ponto in Minnesota on several occasions. Unfortunately fishing was not something our mother was fond of but at Lake Ponto several church families from Omaha had cabins, i.e., Ted Houston's and Frank Heinisch's, which made for a more settling atmosphere (on another note, our mother could always make the best bacon and egg breakfast on the cabin's wood fire stove). He would take the boys fishing along the Missouri River, sometimes overnight, using trotlines and cane fishing poles. He had also taken a few trips to Canada fishing with his 'hunting' buddies; however, tales from these trips remained somewhat guarded. He was a true dad when out hunting and fishing, always safety first, a lot of fun, and many stories to boot. The 1973 and 1974 hunting seasons were quite memorable (I had just gotten out of the service in 1973) and we would talk about these often up until his last few days. He was always interested in my hunting trips, especially deer hunting trips, an experience he never had.

**1973 RESIDENT HUNT**
STATE OF NEBRASKA
11-5-73  DATE  508-24-6152 SOCIAL SECURITY NO.  134417
NAME Noble K Wilmot
STREET 1320 So 51 ST.
TOWN Omaha  NE  68106 ZIP
MO. 8 DAY 4 YEAR 1903 SEX m HT. 5 6 WT. 130 HAIR Gry EYES BR DATE OF BIRTH
DEALER Skaggs #126  EXPIRES DEC. 31, 1973

**1969 RESIDENT HUNT**
STATE OF NEBRASKA
DATE Nov-1-1969  146255
NAME Noble Wilmot
STREET 1302 So 51 Ave
TOWN Omaha Nebr 68106 ZIP
MO. 8 DAY 4 YEAR 03 SEX m HT. 5-6 WT. 130 HAIR h EYES BL DATE OF BIRTH
DEALER Brett Drug  EXPIRES DEC. 31, 1969

**RESIDENT HUNT 1967**
STATE OF NEBRASKA
DATE 10-30-67  154854
NAME Noble Wilmot
STREET 1302 So 51 Ave
TOWN Omaha  Nebr STATE  ZIP
AGE 63 SEX M HEIGHT 5 6 WEIGHT 130 COLOR HAIR Grey COLOR EYES Brn
DEALER Britt Neibube Drug  EXPIRES DEC. 31, 1967

RESIDENT **HUNT - 1966**
EXPIRES DEC. 31, 1966
DATE 10-13-66  N⁰ 153932
NAME N. K. Wilmot
STREET 1302 So 51 Ave
TOWN Omaha  STATE Nebr
AGE 63 SEX M HEIGHT 5'6" WEIGHT 130 COLOR HAIR Dark COLOR EYES Brn
DEALER Brandeis
STATE OF NEBRASKA

Respect private property; ask the farmer first.
The State Conservation Commission of Iowa
Certifies that  Noble K. Wilmot
Street 1302 So 51 st City Omaha
State Nebr , is hereby licensed to hunt during the license year ending December 31, 1974, according to State law and departmental rules of the Conservation Commission.
Occupation of Licensee Retired
Issued in Pot County, Date Oct 10, 1974
Dorothy Leimer County Recorder or Deputy
Pottawattamie County Recorder
I accept this license with the under penalty. My signature certifies that all statements contained hereon are true.
Fred A. Priewert
State Conservation Director
No. 17204 $25.00 Non-Resident Hunting License
Age 71 Hgt. 5-6 Wgt. 125
Eyes Br Hair L Sex m
Noble K Wilmot Signature
ORIGINAL 1974

PERMIT DOLLARS BUY INSURANCE ON FUTURE HUNTING AND FISHING
Expires Dec. 31, 1964
DATE 9-30-64  143765
NAME Noble K. Wilmot
STREET 1302 So 51 Ave
TOWN Omaha  Nebr STATE
RESIDENT HUNT
AGE 61 SEX M HEIGHT 5'6" WEIGHT 135 COLOR HAIR Blk COLOR EYES Brn

RESIDENT PERMIT TO HUNT
EXPIRES DECEMBER 31, 1959
NAME N.K. Wilmot  59395
AGE 56 SEX M  19  59  HT. 5 WT. 6 130
COLOR EYES Brn COLOR HAIR grey blk
TOWN Omaha  STREET 1302 So 51 ave
DEALER Rauli  DATE 10/22/59
STATE OF NEBRASKA

MIGRATORY BIRD HUNTING STAMP
VOID AFTER JUNE 30, 1966
$3
U.S. DEPARTMENT OF THE INTERIOR

$3 MIGRATORY BIRD HUNTING STAMP
VOID AFTER JUNE 30,
Noble K Wilmot
U.S. DEPARTMENT OF THE INTERIOR

Noble's various hunting licenses (front and back)

## Softball, Bowling and Golf:

Following Noble's baseball stint in his early years in and around the Grand Pass and Missouri City venues, upon arrival in Omaha he had turned to fast pitch softball. He would pack up Louise and Mary Lu and head to the Falstaff Ballpark at 24th and Vinton Street in South Omaha (across the street from the Falstaff Brewery). The old wooden bleacher ballpark was the stomping grounds for the best fast pitch softball in Omaha during the 1930s and early 1940s (Note: Hall of Fame softball pitcher, Ben Crain was known to have played at Falstaff Park and across the river in Council Bluffs). Once his three sons came along, he was totally supportive of their softball and baseball careers. He was most often found in the dugout keeping the score book and notoriously arguing with the umpire. (Note: All three played on city championship teams in softball, Bob and Keith played baseball at Central High School, and Jim was elected to the Omaha Softball Hall of Fame.)

From a recreational perspective, Noble was also an avid bowler during the 1960s when bowling was at its apex in Omaha, Nebraska. The team Noble bowled with was 'Midwest' Dundee Shade, a local business owned by sponsor and bowler, Bill Christie. Team members included: Noble and son Jim; Walt and Gene Seaman, Robin Hill, Bill Christie, and Frank Grosbeck. Noble took up golf after retiring. The incentive came after he received a set of golf clubs as a retirement gift. He played on several leagues made up of retirees from the Army Corps of Engineers which included the Strnad brothers, Jim and Frank. Having played a few rounds of golf with our dad, observing Noble with golf clubs was a treat in and of itself. He held the driver with a baseball grip and he approached the putting green with a putter held like a croquet mallet. The end score was 'generally' okay; however, he was known for an occasional errant ball now and then, i.e. striking one golfer in the fairway.

## Scottish Rite and Tangier Shriners:

On November 21, 1963, Noble joined the Omaha Scottish Rite and was made a Knight Commander of the Court of Honor. (The Rank and Decoration of Knight Commander of the Court of Honor (KCCH) is conferred by the Supreme Council upon 32° Masons who have rendered commendable service to the Rite. The members who hold it are designated 32° KCCH. Their cap is red with a Passion Cross in the center of the front.) Noble also was member of the Shrine Temple referred to as the Tangier Shriner's organization in Omaha. He took part in many activities such as the annual Shrine Circus and as an official 'Greeter' at local Shrine events. Noble was often referred to as 'Noble' Noble within the Shrine environment. He was a Charter Member of the "100 Million Dollar Club" for "Shriners Hospitals for Crippled Children" which celebrated their fiftieth birthday in 1972. (Information Note. All Shriners are Masons; however, not all Masons are Shriners. Shriners have temples whereas Masons have lodges. The Shriners were formerly known as the Ancient Arabic Order of the Nobles of the Mystic Shrine established in 1870). Two of

Noble's sons, James and Robert, were both Masons; however, James is a Shriner and Robert is a Mason having been a member of the DeMolay's prior to becoming a Mason. (Noble's Shriner information came from a previous resume of life accomplishments).

Noble - Tangier Shriner 'Greeters' - Omaha - 1973

## Noble and Louise's Final Days:

On November 26, 1969, 4:30 A.M., our mother passed-away at the age of 65 years, 3 months. She was buried November 29, 1969, at Hillcrest Cemetery (now West Lawn - Hillcrest Cemetery), 5701 Center Street, Omaha, Nebraska. She died from 'terminal broncho-pneumonia' and 'cancer of the right colon with metastases to liver, abdominal ascites' (as per death certificate number 154477). Her tending physician was our family doctor, Dr. Daniel Miller. Prior to her final hospitalization she had lived with Noble and son Keith at 1302 So. 51st Ave. Her father as noted on the death certificate was James A. Crabtree and her mother was Anna Mary Foley. What was so unfortunate was that Noble had retired in 1969 from the Army Corp. of Engineers (after 40 years of service), which left the two of them little time to enjoy their final years together. (See Omaha World Herald Obituary below).

WILMOT—Mrs. Louise, age 65 years, 1302 S. 51st Ave. Survived by husband, Noble K.; daughter, Mrs. Eugene (Mary Lu) Seaman; sons, James, Robert, Keith; 2 grandchildren, all of Omaha; sisters, Mrs. Edith Miller, Missouri City, Mo., Mrs. Virginia Shockey, Kansas City, Mo., Mrs. Evelyn Rea, Missouri City, Mo.; brothers, Jewell Crabtree, Orrick, Mo., Jack Crabtree, Kansas City, Kans.
Funeral services Saturday, 11 a.m., First Christian Church. Interment Hillcrest Cemetery. Memorials to the Cancer Fund or the First Christian Church.
JOHN A. GENTLEMAN
WESTSIDE CHAPEL
72nd, Western Ave.          391-1664

Mary Louise Crabtree Wilmot - Obituary 1969

OMAHA-DOUGLAS COUNTY HEALTH DEPARTMENT
Division of Vital Statistics
**CERTIFICATE OF DEATH**

151477

TYPE, OR PRINT IN
PERMANENT INK

| DECEASED—NAME | FIRST | | MIDDLE | | LAST | | SEX | | DATE OF DEATH (MONTH, DAY, YEAR) |
|---|---|---|---|---|---|---|---|---|---|
| MARY | | LOUISE | | WILMOT | | Female | | November 26, 1969 |

RACE WHITE, NEGRO, AMERICAN INDIAN, ETC. (SPECIFY) **White** | AGE—LAST BIRTHDAY (YEARS) **65** | UNDER 1 YEAR MOS. DAYS | UNDER 1 DAY HOURS MIN. | DATE OF BIRTH (MONTH, DAY, YEAR) **Aug. 19, 1904** | COUNTY OF DEATH **Douglas**

CITY, TOWN, OR LOCATION OF DEATH **Omaha** | INSIDE CITY LIMITS (SPECIFY YES OR NO) **Yes** | HOSPITAL OR OTHER INSTITUTION—NAME (IF NOT IN EITHER, GIVE STREET AND NUMBER) **Bishop Clarkson Hospital**

STATE OF BIRTH (IF NOT IN U.S.A., NAME COUNTRY) **Missouri** | CITIZEN OF WHAT COUNTRY **U.S.A.** | MARRIED, NEVER MARRIED, WIDOWED, DIVORCED (SPECIFY) **Married** | SURVIVING SPOUSE (IF WIFE, GIVE MAIDEN NAME) **Noble K. Wilmot**

SOCIAL SECURITY NUMBER **505-76-1739** | USUAL OCCUPATION (GIVE KIND OF WORK DONE DURING MOST OF WORKING LIFE, EVEN IF RETIRED) **Housewife** | KIND OF BUSINESS OR INDUSTRY **Home**

RESIDENCE—STATE **Nebraska** | COUNTY **Douglas** | CITY, TOWN, OR LOCATION **Omaha** | INSIDE CITY LIMITS (SPECIFY YES OR NO) **Yes** | STREET AND NUMBER **1302 South 51st Ave**

FATHER—NAME FIRST **James** MIDDLE **A.** LAST **Crabtree** | MOTHER—MAIDEN NAME FIRST **Anna** MIDDLE **Mary** LAST **Foley**

INFORMANT—NAME—RELATIONSHIP **Noble K. Wilmot     husband** | MAILING ADDRESS (STREET OR R.F.D. NO., CITY OR TOWN, STATE, ZIP) **1302 South 51st Ave., Omaha, Nebraska**

PART I. DEATH WAS CAUSED BY: (ENTER ONLY ONE CAUSE PER LINE FOR (a), (b), AND (c))

IMMEDIATE CAUSE (a) **Terminal broncho-pneumonia**

CONDITIONS, IF ANY, WHICH GAVE RISE TO IMMEDIATE CAUSE (a), STATING THE UNDERLYING CAUSE LAST DUE TO, OR AS A CONSEQUENCE OF (b) **Cancer of the right colon with metastases to liver, abdominal ascites.**

DUE TO, OR AS A CONSEQUENCE OF (c)

PART II. OTHER SIGNIFICANT CONDITIONS: CONDITIONS CONTRIBUTING TO DEATH BUT NOT RELATED TO CAUSE GIVEN IN PART I(a) | PART III. IF FEMALE, WAS THERE A PREGNANCY IN THE PAST 3 MONTHS? YES ☐ NO ☒ | AUTOPSY (YES OR NO) **no** | IF YES WERE FINDINGS CONSIDERED IN DETERMINING CAUSE OF DEATH

ACCIDENT, SUICIDE, HOMICIDE, OR UNDETERMINED (SPECIFY) | DATE OF INJURY (MONTH, DAY, YEAR) | HOUR | HOW INJURY OCCURRED (ENTER NATURE OF INJURY IN PART I OR PART II, ITEM 18)

INJURY AT WORK (SPECIFY YES OR NO) | PLACE OF INJURY AT HOME, FARM, STREET, FACTORY, OFFICE BLDG., ETC. (SPECIFY) | LOCATION (STREET OR R.F.D. NO., CITY OR TOWN, STATE)

CERTIFICATION—PHYSICIAN: I ATTENDED THE DECEASED FROM **10 12 65** TO **11 26 69** AND LAST SAW PM/HER ALIVE ON **11 25 69** | DID/DID NOT VIEW THE BODY AFTER DEATH **no** | DEATH OCCURRED AT THE PLACE, ON THE DATE, AND, TO THE BEST OF MY KNOWLEDGE, FROM THE CAUSE(S) STATED HOUR **4:30a**

CERTIFICATION—MEDICAL EXAMINER OR CORONER: ON THE BASIS OF EXAMINATION OF THE BODY AND/OR THE INVESTIGATION, IN MY OPINION, DEATH OCCURRED ON THE DATE AND DUE TO THE CAUSE(S) STATED | HOUR OF DEATH **4:30 A.** **11 26 69** | THE DECEDENT WAS PRONOUNCED DEAD **4:30 A.**

CERTIFIER **Dunlap M. Miller, M. D.** | SIGNATURE *Dan M Miller* | DEGREE OR TITLE | DATE SIGNED (MONTH, DAY, YEAR) **11-20-69**

MAILING ADDRESS **520 Doctors Building** | STREET OR R.F.D. NO. **Omaha** | CITY OR TOWN | STATE **Nebraska** | ZIP **68131**

BURIAL, CREMATION, REMOVAL (SPECIFY) **Burial** | CEMETERY OR CREMATORY—NAME **Hillcrest Memorial Park** | LOCATION CITY OR TOWN **Omaha, Nebraska** | STATE

DATE **Nov. 29, 1969** | FUNERAL HOME **John A. Gentleman Westside Chapel 72nd and Western Omaha, Nebr**

EMBALMER—SIGNATURE & LICENSE NO. **Lloyd E. Bremer 2148** | REGISTRAR—SIGNATURE *A Lindberg MD* | DATE RECEIVED BY LOCAL REGISTRAR **DEC 1 1969**

I hereby certify that the above is a true and correct copy of the Certificate
of Death recorded in the City of Omaha, County of Douglas, State of Nebraska.

Dated this _____ 1st _____ day of _____ December _____ 1969.

*A Lindberg MD*
(Registrar)

Mary Louise Wilmot - Death Certificate

Our father, Noble King Wilmot, died June 14, 1984, 12:42 AM, at the age of 80 years, 10 months. He was buried June 16, 1984, at West Lawn - Hillcrest Cemetery, 5701 Center Street, Omaha, Nebraska. He died from renal failure (kidney failure) due to 'terminal carcinoma pancreas' (pancreatic cancer) (as per death certificate number 222099). Noble lived at the Masonic Manor, 801 South 52$^{nd}$, Omaha, Nebraska, up until his time of death. He had lived at the Masonic Manor since the mid-1970's when he moved from his family's longtime home at 1302 South 51$^{st}$ Avenue, in Omaha. Interestingly, at the time of his death, he had been a Masonic Member for 50 years, 6 months, and 5 days, (December 8, 1933, to June 14, 1984).[103] having recently received his 50-year award from Centennial Lodge # 326, Omaha, Nebraska.

---

[103] Noble's Masonic Member Profile, Nebraska A.F. & A.M.

Noble King Wilmot - Last Photo - 1984

*The Lord is my Shepherd; I shall not want. He maketh me to lie down in green pastures; He leadeth me beside the still waters. He restoreth my soul; He leadeth me in the paths of righteousness for His name's sake.*

*Yea, though I walk through the valley of the shadow of death, I will fear no evil; for Thou art with me; Thy rod and Thy staff they comfort me; Thou preparest a table before me in the presence of mine enemies; Thou anointest my head with oil, my cup runneth over.*

*Surely goodness and mercy shall follow me all the days of my life; and I will dwell in the house of the Lord forever.*

NOBLE K. WILMOT

Born – August 4, 1903
Died – June 14, 1984

Services
Saturday, June 16, 1984
11:00 A. M.
First Christian Church
Officiant
Rev. Frank Everett
Organist – Art Garwood
Soloist – Phyllis Remington

Graveside Masonic Services
Centennial Lodge A.F.& A.M.
Ben Whitbeck W.M.
Hillcrest Memorial Park

Pallbearers
Rudolph Larsen    Dale Spangler
James Strnad      Glen Gladson
Les Ritter       Sidney Price
Honorary Pallbearers
Frank Strnad   Don Glidewell
Kenneth Schenck   Ray Miller
Frank Frost   Loren Otto

222039

| DECEDENT – NAME | FIRST | MIDDLE | LAST | SEX | DATE OF DEATH (Mo., Day, Yr.) |
|---|---|---|---|---|---|
| 1. | Noble | King | Wilmot | 2. M. | 3. June 14, 1984 |

| RACE – (e.g., White, Black, American Indian, etc.) (Specify) | ORIGIN/DESCENT (e.g., Italian, Mexican, German, etc.) (Specify) | AGE – Last Birthday (Yrs.) | UNDER 1 YEAR MOS. DAYS | UNDER 1 DAY HOURS MINS. | DATE OF BIRTH (Mo., Day, Yr.) |
|---|---|---|---|---|---|
| 4. White | 5. English | 6a. 80 | 6b. | 6c. | 7. Aug. 4th 1903 |

| CITY AND STATE OF BIRTH (If not in U.S.A. name country) | CITIZEN OF WHAT COUNTRY | MARRIED, NEVER MARRIED, WIDOWED, DIVORCED (Specify) | NAME OF SPOUSE (If wife, give maiden name) |
|---|---|---|---|
| 8. Fayette, Mo. | 9. USA | 10. Widowed | 11. -- |

| SOCIAL SECURITY NUMBER | USUAL OCCUPATION (Give kind of work done during most of working life, even if retired) | KIND OF BUSINESS OR INDUSTRY | COUNTY OF DEATH |
|---|---|---|---|
| 12. 503-24-6152 | 13a. Construction Inspector | 13b. U.S. Army Corp. of Engineers | 14a. Douglas |

| CITY, TOWN OR LOCATION OF DEATH | INSIDE CITY LIMITS (Specify Yes or No) | HOSPITAL OR OTHER INSTITUTION – Name (If not in either, give street and number) | IF HOSP. OR INST. Indicate DOA, Outpatient/Emer. Rm., Inpatient (Specify) |
|---|---|---|---|
| 14b. Omaha | 14c. yes | 14d. Nebr. Methodist Hospital | 14e. Inpatient |

| RESIDENCE – STATE | COUNTY | CITY, TOWN OR LOCATION | STREET AND NUMBER | INSIDE CITY LIMITS (Specify Yes or No) |
|---|---|---|---|---|
| 15a. Nebr | 15b. Douglas | 15c. Omaha | 15d. 801 So. 52nd | 15e. yes |

| FATHER – NAME FIRST | MIDDLE | LAST | MOTHER – MAIDEN NAME FIRST | MIDDLE | LAST |
|---|---|---|---|---|---|
| 16. James | | Wilmot | 17. Effie | Alice | Sarton |

| WAS DECEASED EVER IN U.S. ARMED FORCES? (Yes, no, or unk) (If yes, give war and dates of service) | INFORMANT – NAME – RELATIONSHIP – MAILING ADDRESS | (STREET OR R.F.D. NO., CITY OR TOWN, STATE, ZIP) |
|---|---|---|
| 18. No | 19. James Wilmot son 6085 Cedar Omaha, Ne 68124 | |

| BURIAL, Cremation, Removal | DATE | CEMETERY OR CREMATORY – NAME | LOCATION CITY OR TOWN | STATE |
|---|---|---|---|---|
| 20a. Burial | 20b. 6/16/84 | 20c. Hillcrest Cemetery | 20d. Omaha, Nebr. | |

| EMBALMER – SIGNATURE & LICENSE NO. | FUNERAL HOME – NAME AND ADDRESS | (STREET OR R.F.D. NO., CITY OR TOWN, STATE, ZIP) |
|---|---|---|
| 21. Mark Huebner 2267 | 22. John A. Gentleman Westside Chapel 72nd & Western | Omaha, Ne 68114 |

To be Completed by Attending PHYSICIAN Only

| 23a. DATE OF DEATH (Mo., Day, Yr.) June 14, 1984 | | |
|---|---|---|
| 23b. DATE SIGNED (Mo., Day, Yr.) June 22, 1984 | 23c. HOUR OF DEATH 12:42 AM M | |
| 23d. To the best of my knowledge, death occurred at the time, date and place and due to the cause(s) stated. (Signature and Title) /s/ David S. Weeks, M.D. | | |

To be Completed by CORONER'S PHYSICIAN or COUNTY ATTORNEY only

| 24a. DATE SIGNED (Mo., Day, Yr.) | 24b. HOUR OF DEATH M |
|---|---|
| 24c. PRONOUNCED DEAD (Mo., Yr.) | 24d. PRONOUNCED DEAD (Hour) M |
| 24e. On the basis of examination and/or investigation, in my opinion death occurred at the time, date and place and due to the cause(s) stated. (Signature and Title) ▶ | |

NAME AND ADDRESS OF CERTIFIER (PHYSICIAN, CORONER'S PHYSICIAN OR COUNTY ATTORNEY) (Type or Print)

25. David S. Weeks, M.D. 8258 Hascall St., Omaha, Nebr.

REGISTRAR

26a. (Signature) ▶ Daniel J. Korthing, M.P.H.

| DATE RECEIVED BY REGISTRAR (Mo., Day, Yr.) |
|---|
| 26b. JUN 27 1984 |

| 27. IMMEDIATE CAUSE PART (ENTER ONLY ONE CAUSE PER LINE FOR (a), (b), AND (c)) | Interval between onset and death |
|---|---|
| (a) Renal failure | 7 days |
| DUE TO, OR AS A CONSEQUENCE OF: | Interval between onset and death |
| (b) Terminal carcinoma pancreas | 6 months |
| DUE TO, OR AS A CONSEQUENCE OF: | Interval between onset and death |
| (c) | |

| PART II OTHER SIGNIFICANT CONDITIONS – Conditions contributing to death but not related | PART III IF FEMALE, WAS THERE A PREGNANCY IN THE PAST 3 MONTHS? Yes ☐ No ☐ | AUTOPSY (Specify Yes or No) 28. No | WAS CASE REFERRED TO MEDICAL EXAMINER OR CORONER (Specify Yes or No) 29. |
|---|---|---|---|

| ACCIDENT, SUICIDE, HOMICIDE, UNDET. OR PENDING INVESTIGATION (Specify) | DATE OF INJURY (Mo., Day, Yr.) | HOUR OF INJURY | DESCRIBE HOW INJURY OCCURRED |
|---|---|---|---|
| 30a. | 30b. | 30c. M | 30d. |

| INJURY AT WORK (Specify Yes or No) | PLACE OF INJURY – At home, farm, street, factory, office building, etc. (Specify) | LOCATION | STREET OR R.F.D. No. | CITY OR TOWN STATE |
|---|---|---|---|---|
| 30e. | 30f. | 30g. | | |

Noble King Wilmot - Death Certificate

## WILLIAM HOWARD WILMOT

## (Uncle) (1906-1939)

William Howard Wilmot, 'Little Bill', was born January 18, 1906, in Fayette, Howard County, Missouri, to James A. and Effie Alice Sartain Wilmot(t). (Note: William's death certificate indicates a birth date of January 14, 1906; however, a previous personal history statement and driver's license indicate January 18, 1906 as his birth date.) William's mother Effie Alice is assumed to have died sometime between his birth in 1906 and approximately 1909 or 1910 when America P. Sartain (William's grandmother) took William and his two brothers, Orville P. and Noble K. to Cuervo, Guadalupe County, New Mexico. The 1910 United Census for Guadalupe County, New Mexico, identifies the three boys as ages 7, 6 and 4. We do know that the three boys and America P. were in New Mexico for at least two years before they headed back to their home in Missouri. (For more detailed information regarding America P. and Cuervo, New Mexico, - reference the section for Noble K. and his early history). According to William's personal history statement, he had noted that, "I am somewhat hunch back, caused from an injury when three years old." However, William also stated that he was "very active" and had "coached athletics in high school." This explains his documented height in 1936 as between 4'7" and 4'8," weight 100 lbs. His death certificate which referenced scoliosis of the spinal cord may have been the result of his early childhood injury (*see* below death certificate). Not much is known about William's early days after he left Cuervo, New Mexico, with America P. Sartain. However, in 1920, we know from the U.S. Census (January 8, 1920) that William, age 13, was living with his dad and two brothers in Lafayette, Middleton Township, Missouri, and at the time, he was attending school. William H. attended grade school in several school districts: Grand Pass Public Schools, Saline County Public Schools, and Lafayette County Public Schools. (See below William's 7th grade Teacher's Report to Parent). He graduated high school from the Grand Pass Consolidated Schools in 1925. Graduating commencement exercises were held on Thursday evening, May 14, 8:00 o'clock, at the Methodist Church in Grand Pass. The 1925 class consisted of seven students of which William was the class Valedictorian. His classmates included: Arthur Henry Wehnhoener, Lillie Clara Holtz, Ernest Edwin Jones, Archa McReynolds, Josie Helen Coad, and Vera Marguerite Fenner. J. Olan Markland was the Superintendent. The class flower was the white carnation and the class colors were gray and crimson. Interestingly, the class motto was, "Tonight we launch – where shall we anchor."

At the close of each school month, this report will be sent to you for inspection. The exact attitude of your child is marked (X) on the preceding page. I hope you will give it the most careful attention and if anything is unsatisfactory, your encouragement of the child for better work will greatly increase his interest. It is well to consult with the teacher on the marks that are unsatisfactory.

The influence of the home and the school must work toward the same end; that of doing the greatest good for each child. As a teacher, I shall do all in my power for my pupils, and ask you to frequently visit the school, for your presence would be an inspiration and help to both pupils and teacher.

*Oyda M. Grew* Teacher

## SIGNATURE OF PARENT

### HAVE EXAMINED THIS QUARTER'S REPORT

1st Quarter *J. A. Wilmot*

2nd Quarter *J. A. Wilmot*

3rd Quarter *J. A. Wilmot*

4th Quarter

## Certificate of Promotion

### THIS CERTIFIES THAT

*William Wilmott*

has completed the work of the preceding grade and is hereby promoted to the *8th* grade of the Public Schools of this County

*May 7,* 19 *20*

*Mrs. Ed. M. Clure* Teacher

"Kind words are the music of the world." —*Faber.*
"The first step to greatness is to be honest." —*Johnson.*

---

BETTER SCHOOLS

LAFAYETTE COUNTY

# PUBLIC SCHOOLS

## Teacher's Report to Parent

Name *William Wilmot*

District *6* Grade *7*

County *Lafayette* State *Mo.*

For school year ending 19

*Oyda M. K.* Teacher

### If You Wish to Succeed in Life

| Be Cautious | Be Neat | Be Kind |
| Be Faithful | Be Honest | Be True |
| Be Industrious | Be Just | Be Courteous |

*Elmer H. White*

County Superintendent

Front and back of Teacher's Report to Parent for William Wilmot

103

| STUDIES | I | II | III | IV |
|---|---|---|---|---|
| Spelling | E- | E- | 1. | 1 |
| Reading | E- | E- | 2. | 1 |
| Writing | S- | S | 2. | 2 |
| Arithmetic | E | E- | 2. | 1. |
| Language | E- | E- | 1 | |
| Grammar | | | 1 | 1 |
| Geography | S+ | S+ | 2. | 2. |
| U. S. History & Gov't | E- | E- | 1 | 1. |
| Physiology | S+ | E- | | |
| Agriculture | | | 1 | 1 |
| Drawing | | | 2. | 2. |
| *Deportment* | 87 | 80 | 2. | 1 |
| Home Work Credit | S+ | S+ | | |
| Days Present | 40 | 40 | 40 | 40. |
| Days Absent | 1 | 0 | 0 | 0 |
| Times Tardy | 0 | 0 | 0 | 0 |

GRADE } EXCELLENT 90 to 100 GOOD 80 to 90 FAIR 70 to 80 UNSATISFACTORY 60 to 70 POOR Below 60

E + E + S+ - S - M + M - 9 - 8 + 7

| TRAITS OF PUPIL | | | | |
|---|---|---|---|---|
| ATTITUDE TOWARD SCHOOL WORK | Note— Place mark (X) each quarter opposite trait to which attention is called. | | | |
| | I | II | III | IV |
| Indolent | | | | |
| Wastes Time | | X | X | |
| Work is Carelessly Done | some X | | X | |
| Copies | | | | |
| Gives up too Easily | | | | |
| Shows Improvement | \ | | | |
| Very Commendable | | | | |
| RECITATIONS | | | | |
| Comes Poorly Prepared | | | | |
| Appears not to Try | | | | |
| Seldom Does Well | | | | |
| Promotion in Danger | | | X | |
| Capable of doing Better | | | X | |
| Work Shows Falling off | | | | |
| Inattentive | | | | |
| Shows Improvement | X | X | | |
| Very Satisfactory | | | | |
| CONDUCT | | | | |
| Inclined to Mischief | X | X | X | |
| Annoys Others | X | | | |
| Whispers Too Much | | | | |
| Restless | | | | |
| Shows Improvement | | | | |
| Very Good | | | | |

"The young man who smokes cigarettes need not worry about the future; he has none."—*David Starr Jordan.*

'Studies' and 'Traits of Pupil' for William Wilmot, May 7, 1920

After graduating from high school, William enrolled at the University of Missouri in September 1925. He was originally admitted to the College of Engineering; however, during his tenure as a student he changed his focus to both Education and Business Administration. After completing three years at the university, William took a one-year hiatus and became the High School Principal at Arrow Rock, Missouri. The Arrow Rock School Board had hired William for the September 1929 to May 1930 school year at $110.00 per month. William would have been familiar with the Arrow Rock area in Missouri since it was only 32 miles from his hometown of Fayette, Missouri, and approximately 43 miles from the university in Columbia. Williams' time in Arrow Rock was substantiated by the 15th United States Census. The national census for Arrow Rock Township was taken and recorded by Edith Grier on April 29, 1930. The census indicates that William was living in Arrow Rock on Main Street as a boarder with Maybelle P. Biggs, a widow, age 43, and head of household. She was a hostess at a local tavern. William was 23 at the time and, according to the census, he was employed as the Principal at the Arrow Rock 'Public School'. In addition, both of William's parents, James A. and Effie Alice, were noted in the census as being born in Missouri.

After the one-year stint at Arrow Rock high school, William completed his fourth year of college in May 1931, graduating with two degrees, a Bachelor of Science Degree in Education and a Bachelor of Science Degree in Business Administration (*see* below). Diplomas for both degrees were presented to William Howard Wilmot, June 3, 1931. In addition, during the same graduation ceremony in Columbia, Missouri, William received his permanent, 'Life' Teacher's Certificate to teach in the Public Schools of Missouri. During William's tenure at the University of Missouri, he was a member of the Missouri State Teachers Association, a member of the debate squad, and he was awarded the Curators Scholarship. His two bachelor's degrees consisted of 149 credit hours. In addition to William's prerequisite credit hours, his major course of study in business administration consisted of 45 total credits comprised of concentrations in accounting, economics, and finance. His education major consisted of 68 credit hours focusing on specialties which included education, science, and mathematics. And finally, he noted he was familiar with both the typewriter and 'calculating machines.' All in all, a great accomplishment.

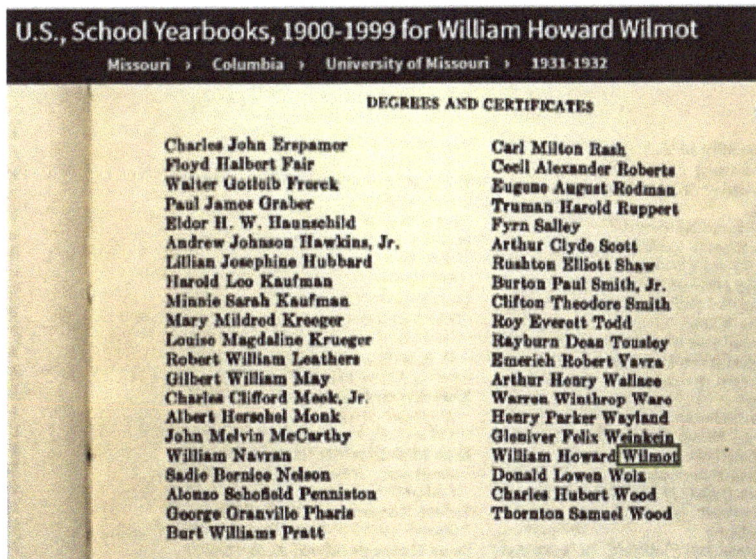

U.S., School Yearbooks, 1900-1999 for William Howard Wilmot
Missouri › Columbia › University of Missouri › 1931-1932

DEGREES AND CERTIFICATES 3

Charles John Erspamer
Floyd Halbert Fair
Walter Gotlieb Frerek
Paul James Graber
Eldor H. W. Haunschild
Andrew Johnson Hawkins, Jr.
Lillian Josephine Hubbard
Harold Leo Kaufman
Minnie Sarah Kaufman
Mary Mildred Kreeger
Louise Magdaline Krueger
Robert William Leathers
Gilbert William May
Charles Clifford Meek, Jr.
Albert Herschel Monk
John Melvin McCarthy
William Navran
Sadie Bernice Nelson
Alonzo Schofield Penniston
George Granville Pharis
Burt Williams Pratt

Carl Milton Rash
Cecil Alexander Roberts
Eugene August Rodman
Truman Harold Ruppert
Fyrn Salley
Arthur Clyde Scott
Rushton Elliott Shaw
Burton Paul Smith, Jr.
Clifton Theodore Smith
Roy Everett Todd
Rayburn Dean Tousley
Emerich Robert Vavra
Arthur Henry Wallace
Warren Winthrop Ware
Henry Parker Wayland
Gleniver Felix Weinkein
William Howard Wilmot
Donald Lowen Wolz
Charles Hubert Wood
Thornton Samuel Wood

Commencement, 1931, University of Missouri
School of Business and Public Administration
Degree of Bachelor of Science in Business Administration (B.S. in Bus. Admin.)

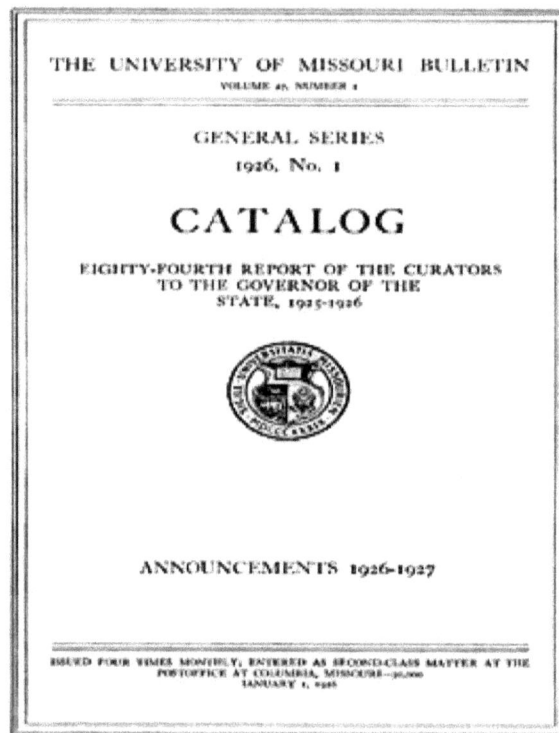

THE UNIVERSITY OF MISSOURI BULLETIN
VOLUME 26, NUMBER 1

GENERAL SERIES
1926, No. 1

# CATALOG

EIGHTY-FOURTH REPORT OF THE CURATORS
TO THE GOVERNOR OF THE
STATE, 1925-1926

ANNOUNCEMENTS 1926-1927

ISSUED FOUR TIMES MONTHLY, ENTERED AS SECOND-CLASS MATTER AT THE
POSTOFFICE AT COLUMBIA, MISSOURI—30,000
JANUARY 1, 1926

## CURATORS' SCHOLARSHIPS[104]

HONOR GRADUATES: The Board of Curators, in an attempt to encourage higher scholarship, offers annually to the honor graduate, or the student attaining the highest scholastic rank in the graduating class of each of the following fully accredited Missouri colleges and schools, a scholarship amounting to exemption for the first two semesters, from the Library, Hospital and Incidental fee. To obtain the scholarship the student must enroll in the University within two years after graduation from the school in which the scholarship was earned and the scholarship must be completely used during the two-year period. Certification of the student's attainment is to be made by the proper official of the institution to the Secretary of the Board of Curators on forms furnished by the latter.

Secondary Schools: All fully accredited secondary schools. Honor graduates of the following schools were awarded Curators' Scholarships during the session of 1925-26:

---

[104] University of Missouri Course Catalogs, 1920-1929 (MU). Announcements 1926-1927. Retrieved from https://mospace.umsystem.edu/xmlui/handle/10355/63024.

| | |
|---|---|
| Eolia | Margaret D. Beall |
| Flat River (class of 1924) | Francis A. Thompson |
| Grand Pass | William Howard Wilmot |
| Greenfield | Carl Courtney |
| Hallsville | Hulett Cooper |
| Holden | Homer E. Raber |
| Hollister (School of the Ozarks) | Jefferson Davis Reagan |
| Houston | Rupert Bridges |
| Houstonia (Consolidated) | Elizabeth Allen Parkhurst |

## Historic Note: Arrow Rock:[105]

William's role as a school Principal and later as a Superintendent of the Arrow Rock school system would have had a brief, but historical impact on the small town of Arrow Rock. Today, Arrow Rock is a village in Saline County, Missouri, located near the Missouri River. The entire village is part of the National Historic Landmark Arrow Rock Historic District, designated by the Department of the Interior, National Park Service in 1963. (Note: the name Arrow Rock was named for the flint from the bluffs which early Native Americans used for their arrows. Early Native Americans in 'Arrow Rock Country' included the Osage and Missouria Indians).

Arrow Rocks' history begins as early as 1723 when French Cartographers, while mapping the Missouri River, marked the location as Pierre a Fleche (Arrow Rock). Lewis and Clark made note of Arrow Rock in 1804 while heading up-river on their infamous expedition. A ferry was established in 1811 across the Missouri River from neighboring towns such as Franklin, Missouri, in Howard County. Stephen H. Long's expedition to Yellowstone passed through in 1818. In 1821, William Becknell, "the Father of the Santa Fe Trail," began his first 800-mile trading journey, by crossing the river from Franklin to Arrow Rock and from there westward to Santa Fe. Thus, the Franklin/Arrow Rock connection became the Eastern departure for the Santa Fe Trail. In 1829 Arrow Rock was officially founded or platted and originally known as 'New Philadelphia' but by 1833 the name returned to its original descriptive name of Arrow Rock. The village took off as a bustling community both for wagon trains heading west on the Santa Fe Trail, the first of the great transcontinental trails and also, where steamboats stopped by on their way west or to unload cargoes of building materials for homes being built in central Missouri. Interestingly, the

---

[105] Hamilton, J. T. (1972). Arrow Rock, Where Wheels Started West. Compiled for The Friends of Arrow Rock, Inc., Guard Printing and Publishing Company, Centralia, Missouri.

eastern half of this trail from the young metropolis of St. Louis to Boone's Lick Country, across the river from Arrow Rock in Howard County, was known as the Boone's Lick Road. After crossing the Missouri River to 'Arrow Rock Country,' the trail westward was known as the Santa Fe Trail. (Note: After the Santa Fe Trail was established, in time, it merged with other renowned trails, i.e., California, Oregon, and Overland trails located west of the Missouri border.) After the Civil War, prosperity returned in a limited fashion. Fires in 1873 and 1901 nearly destroyed the business district of the town. Although a few buildings were rebuilt, times had changed. The Frontier had moved westward, the Santa Fe Trail was only a name, railroads and major highways bypassed the area.

As we know, William's dad, James A., came to the Boone's Lick area in 1880 and was certainly familiar with the Arrow Rock area prior to Williams' arrival. James A. was probably familiar with the Santa Fe Trail having grown up with the Carson family. We do know that Kit Carson traveled the Santa Fe Trail often to his home in Taos, New Mexico. The population of Arrow Rock peaked in 1860 at 1,000. The 1880 Arrow Rock census was 304 with 51% of the population African American, of which most were former plantation slaves. The 1930 census maintained a similar number of residents at 304 with 45% of the population being African American. Today, there is an approximate population of 56 which is all White. The education system of Arrow Rock was divided with African American and White populations having their own schools in 1930. Schools in Arrow Rock eventually became integrated which continued through the late 1950s when the last of the African American students attended school.[106] It would be interesting to know more regarding the role William played in the diverse school system. To that end, further research is ongoing. Thus, for now, we rely on information gained from the 15th United States Census and, William's reporting of his employment as Principal (1929-1930) and Superintendent (1933-1935) of the Arrow Rock school system.

After graduation from college, from September 1931 to September 1933, William worked for the Kansas City Star (newspaper) as a local representative and he did general office work for the Grand Pass Elevator Company. Beginning September 1933, William took a position offered by the Arrow Rock School Board as the High School Superintendent in Arrow Rock, Missouri. The high school superintendent position lasted for two years through May 1935. For the next two years, William worked varied jobs and again, probably due to the after effect of the Great Depression. During the summers of 1935 through 1937 he worked for the P.D. Blake Grain and Feed Company, Waverly, Missouri, as a scale master purchasing and testing grain in addition to general office work. In the fall of 1936, he was employed by the National Re-employment Service, Keytesville, Missouri, as an office manager and interviewer at $70.00 per month. (Note: The

---

[106] Kremer, G. R. (2014). Race and Meaning: The African American Experience in Missouri. The Curators of the University of Missouri. The University of Missouri Press; Columbia, Missouri.

National Re-employment Service was established by the Wagner-Peyser Act of 1933. The law authorized the federal government to cooperate with the states in establishing and maintaining public employment services. Its functions were to develop a national system of public employment offices, furnish information on employment opportunities, and maintain a system for dealing with labor among the states.)[107] Most interesting, according to his personal history statement, as of November 1936, he 'planned to marry this year.' Unfortunately, to date, we have no knowledge as to who his bride-to-be was.

William's application to the Social Security Board in November 1936, included five references which included the following: Roy Emerson Curtis (1886-1960), Dean of Business Administration, University of Missouri, Columbia, MO. Curtis was professor of finance and economics at the University of Missouri and served as Dean of the School of Business Administration through 1942. Dr. Curtis received his A. B. (Bachelor of Arts) from Nebraska Wesleyan in 1907, and his Ph.D. from Wisconsin in 1912.[108] H. G. Brown, professor of economics, University of Missouri. Brown was *Acting* Dean for the School of Business Administration from 1934-1936 and from 1942-1946.[109] Also, Dr. B.C. Bradshaw (1861-1950), Arrow Rock School Board and County Coroner (Saline County); W.F. Rohn, grain dealer, Grand Pass, Missouri; and, Amanda K. Spotts, Postmistress, Grand Pass, Missouri.

Following the summer of 1937, William began work at the Social Security Commission, Accounts and Audits Bureau on January 3, 1938, as an Assistant Auditing Clerk with an annual salary of $1,620.00. The Social Security Commission was located at 412 East High Street, Jefferson City, Missouri. Later that year, on May 25, 1938, William obtained a State of Missouri driver's license (license no. 1056221, *see* below). The driver's license indicated an address of 109 East Miller, Jefferson City, Missouri, and identified his physical characteristics as 31 years of age, white, male, weight:100 lbs., height: 4'7", blue eyes, and sandy hair (the blue eyes and sandy hair were in contrast to Noble K.'s brown eyes and dark brown hair). The assumption is that William obtained the driver's license in tandem with the purchase of a 1931 Model A Ford Coupe for transportation to his next job assignment with the Social Security Commission. On February 13, 1939, William reported for a temporary assignment with the Social Security Commission, Bureau of Accounts and Audits, in Oklahoma City, Oklahoma. Upon arrival, he acquired a State of Oklahoma Operator's License (license no. 782058), which hints of travel by car, most likely, with his 1931 Model A Ford. (Note: We do not know the reason William left Jefferson City for a 'temporary' job in Oklahoma although perhaps both positions may have been 'temporary'.)

[107] U.S. Department of Labor. Wagner-Peyser Act Employment Service Results. Retrieved from https://www.dol.gov/agencies/eta/performance/results/wagner-peyser.
[108] The State Historical Society of Missouri. (2019). Roy Emerson Curtis Papers, 1935-1940. Retrieved from https://collections.shsmo.org/manuscripts/columbia/c3408.pdf.
[109] University of Missouri. (2019). Robert J. Trulaske Jr., College of Business. Retrieved from https://business.missouri.edu/about-trulaske/history.

Unfortunately, on May 12, 1939, William was separated from service 'without prejudice.' His separation from service was caused by the 'expiration' of his 'temporary' appointment. (Note: Once William obtained employment with the Social Security Commission in 1938, he extended goodwill to his father, James A., by taking control of his father's farm and providing James A. a home without any encumbrances for the rest of his life. For full details, *see* the '1930' section for James A. previously described).

It is uncertain if William was employed after he departed Oklahoma City and returned to Missouri. He passed-away at 12:20 a.m. on November 28, 1939, at St. Joseph's Hospital, Boonville, Missouri. (Our mother died on November 26, 1969, however, other than our dad, no one realized their deaths were two days apart in the month of November.) His Missouri death certificate, 39418, stated that at the time of death, he was a 'Teacher' and had been for three years.[110] William's cause of death was acute bronchitis with his scoliosis of the spinal cord as a contributing factor. His burial occurred in Grand Pass, Missouri, on November 29, 1939; however, we have no information as to which cemetery. (Similarly, William's dad, James A., was buried at Grand Pass, Missouri. Cemetery unknown.)

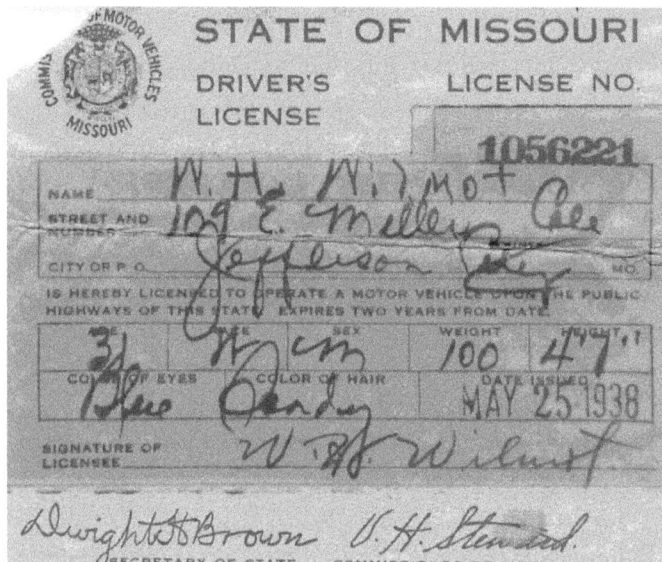

W. H. Wilmot State of Missouri Driver's License - 1938

---

[110] William Howard Wilmot. (2015). Missouri, Death Certificates, 1910-1962. Missouri State Board of Health, Certificate of Death-39418. Ancestry.com.

Soon after William's death, on December 19, 1939, Noble K. received correspondence from the University of Missouri. The letter stated that the university had received a check for $1,511.51, from the Metropolitan Life Insurance Company on the life of William Wilmot, which was applied as full settlement for William's student loan funds. The remaining $86.58 interest was charged off. Thus, his indebtedness to the university was paid in full.

On January 20, 1940, Noble K. received an interesting letter from Robert E. Bridwell, Jr., Auditor-in-Charge, Oklahoma City, Oklahoma, Social Security Board, which explained the details of William's separation from service. Bridwell followed by extending the commission's condolences, "We were indeed sorry to hear that 'Willie' had passed on as he was well liked by all of the boys that worked with him." Another interesting communication regarding William was posted to Noble K. via Western Union on February 8, 1941. The unsuccessful Western Union telegram delivery to William H. Wilmot stated, "Would you accept permanent appointment as Senior Account Clerk in Jefferson City Office of Social Security Commission at $125 per month if selected. Wire reply immediately. William G. Colman, Merit System Supervisor." Obviously, William was well thought of by the Social Security Commission and by his early passing, he unfortunately missed a great opportunity.

**MISSOURI STATE BOARD OF HEALTH**
BUREAU OF VITAL STATISTICS
CERTIFICATE OF DEATH

**39418**
Do not use this space.

1. PLACE OF DEATH
(a) County COOPER
Registration District No. 218
(b) Township
Primary Registration District No. 3015
(c) City BOONVILLE
(d) Street No. ST. JOSEPH'S HOSPITAL St.
(If death occurred in Hospital or Institution, write its name instead of street and number)
Registered No. 126
(e) Length of residence in city or town where death occurred 453 yrs. mos. ds. (f) How long in U.S., if of foreign birth? yrs. mos. ds.

2. PRINT FULL NAME WILLIAM HOWARD WILMOT
(a) Residence, No. GRAND PASS, MO. St.
(Usual place of abode, if no street address, write county or city)
(If nonresident, give city or town and State)

| PERSONAL AND STATISTICAL PARTICULARS | MEDICAL CERTIFICATE OF DEATH |
|---|---|
| 3. SEX MALE  4. COLOR OR RACE WHITE  5. SINGLE, MARRIED, WIDOWED, OR DIVORCED (write the word) SINGLE | 21. DATE OF DEATH (MONTH, DAY, AND YEAR) Nov 28, 1939 |
| 5A. IF MARRIED, WIDOWED, OR DIVORCED HUSBAND OF (OR) WIFE OF SINGLE | 22. I HEREBY CERTIFY, That I attended deceased from Nov 20, 1939, to Nov 28, 1939. I last saw him alive on Nov 28, 1939. Death is said to have occurred on the date stated above, at 12 a. m. |
| 6. DATE OF BIRTH (MONTH, DAY, AND YEAR) JAN 14 1906 | The principal cause of death and related causes of importance were as follows: |
| 7. AGE YEARS 33  MONTHS 10  DAYS 14  If LESS than 1 day ...hrs. or ...min. | acute bronchitis  8/h  Date of onset |
| 8. Trade, profession, or particular kind of work done, as sawyer, bookkeeper, etc. SCHOOL | |
| 9. Industry or business in which work was done, as saw mill, bank, etc. TEACHER | |
| 10. Date deceased last worked at this occupation (month and year) NOV 1939  11. Total time (years) spent in this occupation 3 YRS | |
| 12. BIRTHPLACE (CITY OR TOWN) (STATE OR COUNTRY) HOWARD COUNTY MISSOURI | Other contributory causes of importance: |
| FATHER 13. NAME JAMES A. WILMOT | Name of operation ... Date of ... |
| 14. BIRTHPLACE (CITY OR TOWN) (STATE OR COUNTRY) NEW YORK | What test confirmed diagnosis? ... Was there an autopsy? No |
| MOTHER 15. MAIDEN NAME EFFIE A SARTAN | 23. If death was due to external causes (violence), fill in also the following: Accident, suicide, or homicide? ... Date of injury ..., 19 |
| 16. BIRTHPLACE (CITY OR TOWN) (STATE OR COUNTRY) HOWARD COUNTY MISSOURI | Where did injury occur? (Specify city or town, county, and State) |
| 17. INFORMANT NOBLE WILMOT (ADDRESS) OMAHA NEBRASKA | Specify whether injury occurred in industry, in home, or in public place. |
| 18. BURIAL, CREMATION, OR REMOVAL PLACE GRAND PASS DATE NOV 29 1939 | Manner of injury  Nature of injury |
| 19. FUNERAL DIRECTOR (NAME) STEGNER-KOENIG (ADDRESS) BOONVILLE MO. | 24. Was disease or injury in any way related to occupation of deceased? No If so, specify |
| 20. FILED 11-28 1939 ___ Hooper  Local Registrar. | (Signed) O. H. Van Ravenswaay M.D.  (Address) Boonville Mo. 197 |

(Licensed Embalmer's Statement on Reverse Side)

William Howard Wilmot - Death Certificate - Missouri - 39418

# ORVILLE PRICE WILMOT

## (Uncle) 1902-1986

Orville was born May 26, 1902, in Fayette, Howard County, Missouri. He died September 21, 1986, in Grandview, Jackson County, Missouri, at the age of 84. Orville is buried at Mount Olivet (Catholic) Cemetery and Mausoleum, Kansas City, Jackson County, Missouri. Orville was married to Bessie Audry (Baldwin) Wilmot, born February 18, 1908, and died October 17, 2002, at the age of 94. Bessie was buried at Mount Olivet Cemetery, Kansas City, Missouri, along-side Orville. (Note: After their brother, William Howard, and their father, James A., died in 1939 and 1941 respectfully, there was little, if any, family contact between Orville and Noble's families. Unfortunately, we never met our uncle Orville or his wife Bessie. However, as an end note, Orville's family, specifically the Steve Williamson family, have done fantastic research on their family history located at Ancestry.com., so we will not pursue Orville's family in further detail.)

## Additional Photographs:

All family historians understand the importance of documenting and preserving the history of our past. Photographs are but one way to do so. The following photographs of dad and family present an array of time endeared moments which enable us to draw closer to our ancestral family, to better our understanding of their lives, and to provide us a sense of belonging to something bigger than ourselves.

Mom and Dad - Christmas - 1954

Mom and Dad - 1958

Mom, Bob, and Dad - Vacation - Itasca
State Park, Mississippi River Headwaters
1962

Dad and Jim - Bowling Team - 1963

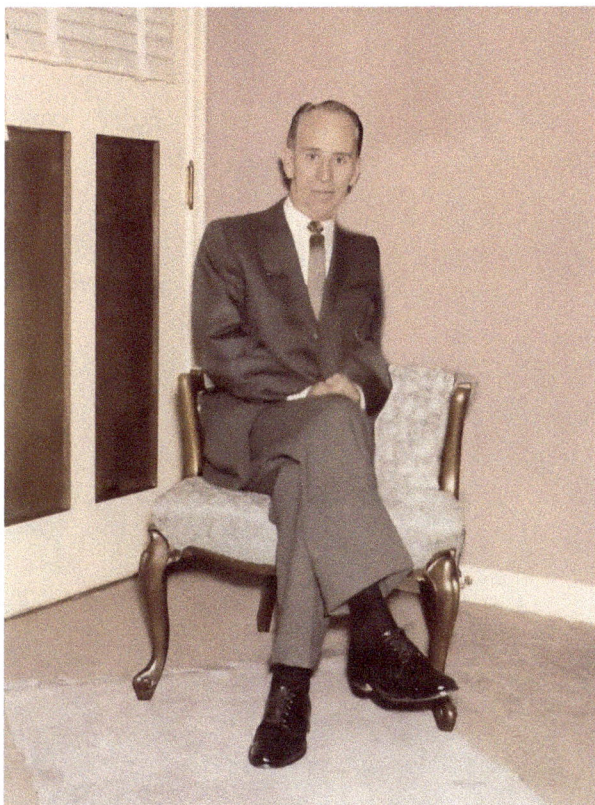

Noble K. Wilmot - 1962

Noble K. Wilmot - 1971

Left to Right: Bob, Keith, Mary Lu and Jim Wilmot - Circa 1950

# REFERENCES

Acadia, Canada, Vital and Church Records. *Drouin Collection*. 1757-1946. (2007). Digital Images. Ancestry.com.

Atchison, A. (1937). Place Names of Five West Central Counties of Missouri. M.A. thesis., University of Missouri-Columbia.

Australian Dictionary of Biography. (1966). Sir Robert Wilmot Horton (1784-1841). Retrieved from http://adb.anu.edu.au/biography/horton-sir-robert-wilmot-2199.

Bardsley, C. W. (1901) A Dictionary of English and Welsh Surnames. Oxford University Press.

Beau Knot News, 1937, Edition 1, Volume 7, Lamonte Roach, President, and Dr. J.T. Ferguson, Teacher. Kansas City, Missouri.

Calvary Cemetery List of Interments in Section 4, Range 13, Plot D, Grave 15. Digital Images. Ancestry.com.

Camey, L. H. (2016). Atlantic Canada's Irish Immigrants, A Fish and Timber Story. Dundurn Press.

Charles Cline Obituary. (1862, May 1). The New York Herald, page 5. New York, NY: 1840-1920.

Charles Kline. Death Notice. (2018). New York City Department of Records and Information Services. Municipal Archives: New York, NY.

Church Baptism Records. (2017). *Mallow Heritage Centre* (Cork North and East). Retrieved from https://www.rootsireland.ie.

Church Marriage Records July 1794 to November 1794. (2017). *Mallow Heritage Centre* (Cork North and East). Cloyne/Microfilm 04990/01, Page 14. Retrieved from http://www.rootsireland.ie.

Collins, M. (2019). Your Irish Heritage. Correspondence retrieved from http://www.youririshheritage.com.

Costello, A.E. (1997). Our Firemen – A History of the New York Fire Departments, Volunteer and Paid. New York: Knickerbocker Press.

Council Bluffs Nonpareil (Council Bluffs, Iowa). (1956). Online Publication. Digital Images. Ancestry.com (2006). Retrieved from https://www.ancestry.com/interactive/8290/NEWS-IA-CO_BL_IO_NO.1956_03_06_0017/501323793?backurl=https%3a%2f%2fwww.ancestry.com%2ffamilytree%2fperson%2ftree%2f81211940%2fperson%2f260046611370%2ffacts&ssrc=&backlabel=Return.

Cuervo Clipper. The University of New Mexico Digital Repository included issues published between 1/7/1910 through 12/1/1922. Retrieved from https://digitalrepository.unm.edu/cuervo_clipper_news/.

Dickens, C. (2006). American Notes for General Circulation. Echo Library, Teddington, Middlesex, 2006. (Reprint, original published in London, 1850).

Donnelly, J. S. Jr. (2009). Captain Rock: The Irish Agrarian Rebellion of 1821-1824. The University of Wisconsin Press.

Encyclopedia Britannica. (2019). Bounty System. Retrieved from https://www.britannica.com/event/Bounty-System.

Ernst, R. (1994). Immigrant Life in New York City, 1825-1863. Syracuse University Press, Syracuse, New York.

Griffith's Valuation. (2017). Retrieved from http//www.findmypast.com.

Hamilton, J. T. (1972). Arrow Rock, Where Wheels Started West. Compiled for The Friends of Arrow Rock, Inc., Guard Printing and Publishing Company, Centralia, Missouri.
History of Howard and Cooper Counties, Missouri. (2004). Hearthstone Legacy Publications, Missouri.

Hodges, G. R. (2012). New York City Cartmen, 1667-1850. New York: University Press.

Holt, M. I. (1992). The Orphan Trains – Placing Out in America. University of Nebraska Press, Nebraska and London.

Index to Petitions for Naturalizations Filed in Federal, State, and Local Courts in New York City, 1792-1906. (2013). Digital Images. Ancestry.com.

Ireland Catholic Parish Marriage Images. Library of Ireland. Retrieved from http://search/findmypast.com.

James Wilmot (a) Obituary. (1874, August 17). The New York Herald. Digital Images. Library of Congress, Washington, D.C.

James Wilmot (a). New York City Death Certificate 185845. Department of Records and Information Services. Municipal Archives.

James Wilmott (b). Death Notice. New York City Department of Records and Information Services. Municipal Archives: New York, NY.

James A. Wilmot. Missouri State Board of Health, Bureau of Vital Statistics. Certificate of Death 11164.

Kennedy, R.C. (2001). HarpWeek. New York Times. Retrieved from https://archive.nytimes.com/www.nytimes.com/learning/general/onthisday/harp/0414.html.

Keeter, C. (1910). The Cuervo Clipper, 12-02-1910. https://digitalrepository.unm.edu/cuervo_clipper_news/44.

Keeter, C. (1912) The Cuervo Clipper, 08-01-1912. https://digitalrepository.unm.edu/cuervo_clipper_news/88.

Keeter, C. (1912) The Cuervo Clipper, 10-24-1912. https://digitalrepository.unm.edu/cuervo_clipper_news/96.

Kington, D. M. (1995). Forgotten Summers: The Story of the Citizens' Military Training Camps, 1921-1940. Two Decades Publishing, San Francisco, California.

Kremer, G. R. (2014). Race and Meaning: The African American Experience in Missouri. The Curators of the University of Missouri. The University of Missouri Press; Columbia, Missouri.

Library of Congress. (2017). Map of City, New York, Extending North to Fiftieth Street. Surveyed and Drawn by J. F. Harrison, C.E. Published by M. Dripps, 103 Fulton Street and 50 Ann Street, NY, 1852. Retrieved from https://www.loc.gov/item/2017586293/.

MacLysaght, E. (1985). Surnames of Ireland. Irish Academic Press. Kildare, Ireland. Retrieved from www.johngrenham.com.

McKeown, M. (2018). Blood of the Irish: What DNA Tells Us About the People in Ireland. Owlcation – Genetics & Evolution. Retrieved from https://owlcation.com/stem/Irish-Blood-Genetic-Identity.

New York City Department of Records and Information Services. Municipal Archives: 31 Chambers Street, New York, NY.

Maria Willmot Obituary. (1872, September 08). The New York Herald, page 5. Digital Images. Library of Congress, Washington, D.C.

Massachusetts Passenger and Crew List, 1820-1946, for Mary Wilmouth, Roll M277, Arriving at Boston, MA, 1820-1891. (2006). Digital Images. Ancestry.com.

Massman Construction Company. (2020). History. Retrieved from https://www.massman.net/history.

Michael Wilmott Obituary. (1867, May 30). The New York Herald, page 12. New York, NY: 1840-1920. Digital Images. Library of Congress, Washington, D.C.

Michael Wilmot. New York City Death Notices Transcription, 1835-1880. Digital Images. Findmypast.com.

Muriel Wilmot. Certificate of Death 129113. New York City Department of Records and Information Services, Municipal Archives.

National Park Service. (2019) Homestead Act. https://www.nps.gov/home/learn/historyculture/abouthomesteadactlaw.htm.

New York, Immigration and Passenger List, 1820-1850, Ship: *Switzerland*, Family Identification: 117678. Ancestry.com.

NYC: Willett Street Church Baptism and Marriage Records, New York and Vicinity, United Methodist Church Records, 1775-1949. Ancestry.com.

Patrick, D. and Trickel, E. G. (1997). Orphan Trains to Missouri. University of Missouri Press, Columbia and London.

Reagan, T.E. (2005). Images of America - New York Fire Patrol. Arcadia Publishing.

Rockland Lake and the Hudson Valley Ice Industry. (2019). https://hvmag.com/life-style/rockland-lake-and-the-hudson-valley-ice-industry/.

Ruxton, D. (2020). Wakes, beggars and 'bad air': When typhus killed 65,000 people in Ireland. The Irish Times. Retrieved from https://www.irishtimes.com/news/ireland/irish-news/wakes-beggars-and-bad-air-when-typhus-killed-65-000-people-in-ireland-1.4203488.

St-Jean Bureau de Sante, 1831-1832. Acadia, Canada, Vital and Church Records, *Drouin Collection*, 1752-1946. (2007). Digital Images. Ancestry.com.

Sides, H. (2006). Blood and Thunder, An Epic of the American West. Doubleday Publishing, New York.

Sophia Klein. (2003). New York, Immigration and Passenger List, 1820-1850. Ship: *Switzerland*, Family Identification: 117678. Ancestry.com.

Sophia Wilmott/Wilmot. New York City Department of Records and Information Services, Municipal Archives.

Sykes, B. (2006). Saxons, Vikings, and Celts, the Genetic Roots of Britain and Ireland. New York: W.W. Norton and Company.

The State Historical Society of Missouri. (2019). Roy Emerson Curtis Papers, 1935-1940. Retrieved from https://collections.shsmo.org/manuscripts/columbia/c3408.pdf.

U.S. Army Register of Enlistments, 1798-1914. Digital Images. (2007). Ancestry.com.

U. S. City Directories, 1822-1995. (2011). Kansas City, Missouri, City Directory. 1931, 1933. Digital Images. Ancestry.com.

U. S. City Directories, 1822-1995. (2011). Omaha, Nebraska, City Directory. 1938, 1940. Digital Images. Ancestry.com.

U. S. City Directories, 1822-1995. (2011). Patterson, New Jersey, City Directory. 1874. Digital Images. Ancestry.com.

U.S. Department of Labor. Wagner-Peyser Act Employment Service Results. Retrieved from https://www.dol.gov/agencies/eta/performance/results/wagner-peyser.

U.S. World War II Draft Cards Young Men 1940-1947. Digital Images. Ancestry.com. (2011).

Union Historical Company. (1881). The History of Jackson County, Missouri, containing A History of the County, Its Cities, Towns, etc. Birdsall, Williams and Co., Kansas City, MO. Retrieved from https://catalog.hathitrust.org/Record/008653337.

United States Marriages Transcription. Sophia Kline and James Wilmot. Digital Images. Findmypast.com. FamilySearch film number: 001671673.

University of Missouri Course Catalogs, 1920-1929 (MU). Announcements 1926-1927. Retrieved from https://mospace.umsystem.edu/xmlui/handle/10355/63024.

University of Missouri. (2019). Robert J. Trulaske Jr., College of Business. Retrieved from https://business.missouri.edu/about-trulaske/history.

Verstappen, P. (2018). Forebears - Wilmot Surname Meaning. Retrieved from https://forebears.io/surnames/wilmot#meaning.

Walsh, Michael. (2018). MAGI Family Lines. (Independent family research for K. Wilmot). https://www.michael@myirishconnections.com.

Willett Street Methodist Episcopal Church. Retrieved in 2018 from http://daytoninmanhattan.blogspot.com/2015/06/the-1826-willletts-street-methodist.html.

William Howard Wilmot. (2015). Missouri, Death Certificates, 1910-1962. Missouri State Board of Health, Certificate of Death-39418. Ancestry.com.

Winder, G. W. (2000). Trouble in the North End: The Geography of Social Violence in Saint John 1840-1860. *Acadiensis*, Vol. 29, No. 2 Spring, 2000.

# DOCUMENTS

## Children's Aid Society Letter

via email

Bob Wilmot

Re: James Wilmot

June 2, 2015

Dear Bob

On June 4, 1878, James Wilmot came to the Children's Aid Society from the Home of the Friendless. James was age 8 and born on August 28, 1870. He was placed by J.P. Brace of Children's Aid Society with George W. Carson of Boonesboro, MO., in Howard County.

In March 1879 Mr. Carson wrote that James was doing well.
In April 1879, a Mr. Bennett, possibly from the Home of the Friendless, wrote that James was an orphan. One of his parents was American and one German.

March 1881, Mr. Carson wrote to Mr. Brace and requested that Mr. Brace place James in another home.

June 1, 1889, Mr. Carson wrote that James was still in the area. He lived in Sisborn, Howard county, MO.

Sept. 14, 1889, James wrote that Mr. Carson promised him a saddle, a bridle and a good suit of clothes if James stayed until he was 21. Mr. Carson was very hard on him and after 4 years James would not stay and moved to Mr. Hardin Maupin. Mr. Maupin died and James remained with his son James Maupin. James wrote he had not had many advantages and was working for $1.50/day on the river.

Sept. 20, 1889, Mr. Harris of the Home of the Friendless wrote that James Wilmot was surrendered by his Aunt Mrs. Peter Wilmot of 76 Mangin St. New York. Mrs. Wilmot had a large family of her own and was unable to keep him. His father, also named James, and his mother Sophie were both dead. James had a married sister and brother 14 years old but the

Home of the Friendless knew nothing of them. James' father was American and his mother was German. James was brought to the Home of the Friendless March 23, 1878.

In December 28, 1889, James had a good home with W.D. Ainsworth Boonesboro, MO.

April 19, 1890 James wrote that he lived on the farm with Mr. Ainsworth. James was very anxious to learn the whereabouts of his relatives.

June 29, 1895, an attorney from Marshall MO. asked for information on James Wilmot.

*There is no information on why an attorney was seeking information on James or who the attorney was representing.*

Regards,

Paul Clarke
Archives Office
150 East 45 Street, Floor 2
New York, NY 10017
Phone: 212-949-4847

The Children's Aid Society, 150 East 49 Street, New York, NY 10017

# CENSUS INDEX[111]

7th US Census - 1850 - New York, New York

7th US Census - 1850 - Michael Wilmott and Family - New York, New York

---

[111] All United States Census Information was obtained from the National Archives and Records Administration via Ancestry.com. or findmypast.com.

# 1850 US Census Transcription

## Household Members

| First name(s) | Last name | Gender: | Age | Birth year | Birth place |
|---|---|---|---|---|---|
| Michl | Wilmott | Male | 45 | 1805 | Ireland |
| Mary | Wilmott | Female | 45 | 1805 | Ireland |
| Jas | Wilmott | Male | 17 | 1833 | New Brunswick |
| Wm | Wilmott | Male | 15 | 1835 | New Brunswick |
| Ann | Wilmott | Female | 12 | 1838 | New Brunswick |
| Alice | Wilmott | Female | 10 | 1840 | New Brunswick |
| Mary | Wilmott | Female | 8 | 1842 | New Brunswick |
| Peter | Wilmott | Male | 5 | 1845 | New Brunswick |
| John | Wilmott | Male | 3 | 1847 | New Brunswick |

Michael Wilmott Family - 7th US Census - 1850 - New York, New York (Transcript)

# New York, State Census, 1855 for Michael Wilmott

New York › New York City, Ward 13 › E.D. 6

**I. Population.** Census of the Inhabitants in the _Sixth_ Election District of the _Thirteenth Ward_ of _New York_ in the County of _New York_ taken by me on the _Twenty Fifth_ day of June, 1855.

_E. F. Boyd_ Marshal.

| | | | Name of every person whose usual place of abode on the first day of June was in this family. | Age | Sex | Relation to the head of the family | In what county of this State, or in what other State or Foreign Country born | | Years resident in this city | Profession, Trade, or Occupation | | | | | | |
|---|---|---|---|---|---|---|---|---|---|---|---|---|---|---|---|---|
| 43 | | 252 | Henry Dryer | 36 | M | | Germany | 1 | 20 | Shoemaker | 1 | | | | | 1 |
| | | | Frances " | 40 | F | Wife | " | 1 | 20 | | | 1 | | | | 2 |
| | | | Elizabeth " | 1 | " | Child | New York | | 1 | | | | | | | 3 |
| | | | Fredrick Ortmichi | 30 | M | R. D. | Prussia | | 1 ½ | | | | 1 | | | 4 |
| | | 253 | John Colan | 26 | " | | New York | 1 | 26 | Shoemaker | 1 | | | | | 5 |
| | | | Rose " | 25 | F | Wife | Ireland | 1 | 9 | | | 1 | | | | 6 |
| | | | Mary " | 1 | " | Child | New York | 1 | | | | | | | | 7 |
| | | 254 | Joseph Sinkworm | 50 | M | | Germany | 1 | 2 | Watchman | 1 | | | | | 8 |
| | | | Mary " | 44 | F | Wife | " | 1 | 2 | | | 1 | | | | 9 |
| | | | Frances " | 8 | " | Child | New York | | 3 | | | | | | | 10 |
| | | | Mary " | 5 | " | " | " | | 5 | | | | | | | 11 |
| 44 | Brick Tent | 255 | Michael Wilmott | 44 | M | | Ireland | 1 | 14 | Tinsman | 1 | | | | | 12 |
| | | | Mary " | 42 | F | Wife | " | 1 | 14 | | | | | | | 13 |
| | | | Mary A. " | 13 | " | Child | New York | | 13 | | | | | | | 14 |
| | | | Peter " | 11 | M | " | " | | 11 | | | | | | | 15 |
| | | | John " | 7 | " | " | " | | 7 | | | | | | | 16 |
| | | 256 | James Wilmott | 23 | " | | New Brunswick | 1 | 14 | Tinsman | 1 | | | | | 17 |
| | | | Sophia " | 17 | F | Wife | New York | 1 | 17 | | | | | | | 18 |
| | | | William Wilmott | 22 | M | | New Brunswick | 1 | 14 | Tinsman | 1 | | | | | 19 |
| | | | Margaret " | 19 | F | Wife | Ireland | 1 | 7 | | | 1 | | | | 20 |
| | | 257 | Jane Droth | 43 | M | | Germany | 1 | 2 | Laborer | 1 | | | | | 21 |

Michael, James, and William Wilmott Families
New York Census - 1855 - 6th District, 13th Ward, New York, New York

| 27 | | Ellen | " | 3 | F | ✓ | | | | " | " | | | | 27 |
| 28 | | Catherine | " | 5 | F | ✓ | | | | " | " | | 1 | | 28 |
| 29 | 1004 | Francis Wilmot | | 56 | M | ✓ | Truck Driver | | | Ireland | | | | | 29 |
| 30 | | Mary | " | 53 | F | ✓ | | | | " | | | | | 30 |
| 31 | | Peter | " | 14 | M | ✓ | | | | New York | | | 1 | | 31 |
| 32 | | John | " | 11 | M | ✓ | | | | " | " | | 1 | | 32 |
| 33 | 1005 | James Wilmot | | 28 | M | ✓ | Carman | | | " | " | | | | 33 |
| 34 | | Jane | " | 22 | F | ✓ | | | | " | " | | | | 34 |
| 35 | | Alice | " | 1/2 | F | ✓ | | | | " | " | | | | 35 |
| 36 | | Charles Klein | | 24 | M | ✓ | Oysterman | | | " | " | | | | 36 |
| 37 | 267 1006 | Philip Leddy | | 24 | M | ✓ | Clerk | | $300 | Ireland | | | | | 37 |
| 38 | | Catherine | " | 22 | F | ✓ | | | | " | | | | | 38 |
| 39 | 1007 | Bernard Fay | | 35 | M | ✓ | Book Fitter | | | " | | | | | 39 |
| 40 | | Catherine | " | 26 | F | ✓ | | | | " | | | | | 40 |

No. white males, 19   No. colored males, _   No. foreign born, _   No. blind, _
No. white females, 21   No. colored females, _   No. deaf and dumb, _   No. insane, _
No. idiotic, _
No. paupers, _
No. convicts, _

300

James Wilmott Family - 8th US Census - 1860 - District 1, Ward 13, New York, New

Page No. 48

☞ Inquiries numbered 7, 18, and 17 are not to be asked in respect to infants. Inquiries numbered 11, 12, 15, 16, 17, 19, and 20 are to be answered (if at all) merely by an affirmative mark, as /.

SCHEDULE 1.—Inhabitants in 2nd Dis 13 Ward, in the County of New York, State of New York, enumerated by me on the 7 day of January 1870. Eugene Martin Ass't Marshal.

Post Office: New York

| 1 | 2 | 3 | 4 | 5 | 6 | 7 | 8 | 9 | 10 | 11 | 12 | 13 | 14 | 15 16 17 | 18 | 19 | 20 | |
|---|---|---|---|---|---|---|---|---|---|---|---|---|---|---|---|---|---|---|
| 33 | | McCann Mary | 55 | F | | | | | Ireland | | | | | | | | | 1 |
| | | " Ella | 18 | F | | | | | NY | | | | | | | | | 2 |
| | | Wilmot James | 34 | M | | Cartman | | | " | | | | | | | | | 3 |
| | | " Sophia | 33 | F | | | | | " | | | | | | | | | 4 |
| | | " Alice | 11 | F | | | | | " | | | | | | | | | 5 |
| | | " William | 8 | M | | | | | " | | | | | | | | | 6 |
| | | " James | 5 | M | | | | | " | | | | | | | | | 7 |
| | | Burk James | 49 | M | | Boilermaker | | | Ireland | | | | | | | | | 8 |
| | | " Ann | 50 | F | | | | | " | | | | | | | | | 9 |
| | | " John | 13 | M | | | | | NY | | | | | | | | | 10 |
| | | " James | 16 | M | | | | | | | | | | | | | | 11 |

48 of 70

Records Administration

James Wilmot Family
9th US Census - January 7, 1870 - Lewis Street, New York Ward 13, New York, New York

**1870 United States Federal Census for James Willmot**
New York › New York › New York Ward 13 District 10

James Wilmot Family
9th US Census - June 14, 1870 - New York Ward 13, New York, New York

**1880 United States Federal Census for Mary Wilmot**
New York › New York › New York City › 132

10th US Census - 1880 - New York City (Manhattan), New York
Mary (Collan) Wilmot - Great Great Grandmother

James Wilmot (James A. Wilmot and G.W. Carson Family)
10th US Census - 1880 - Boons Lick Township, Howard County, Missouri

James A. 'Wilmoth' - Hired Hand
12th US Census - 1900 - Boons Lick Township, Howard County, Missouri

## 1900 United States Federal Census for Effie Sartain

Missouri › Howard › Chariton › District 0062

| Line Num | Street | House Numb | Num in Order | Family No | Name | Relation to Head | Race | Sex | Birth Month | Birth Year | Age | Marital Status | Years Married | Children | Children | Birthplace | Father's Birthplace | Mother's Birthplace |
|---|---|---|---|---|---|---|---|---|---|---|---|---|---|---|---|---|---|---|
| 25 | | | | | Alexander | Daughter | W | F | ? | 1885 | 14 | S | | | | Missouri | Missouri | Missouri |
| 25 | | | | | , Alexander | Son | W | M | S | ? | 1888 | 12 | S | | | | Missouri | Missouri | Missouri |
| 26 | | 236 | 238 | | Sartain, America | Head | W | F | Oct | 1861 | 38 | Wd | | 3 | 3 | Missouri | Missouri | Kentucky |
| 27 | | | | | , Effie | Daughter | W | F | Sept | 1883 | 16 | S | | | | Missouri | Missouri | Missouri |
| 28 | | | | | , Gracie | Daughter | W | F | June | 1882 | 18 | S | | | | Missouri | Missouri | Missouri |
| 29 | | | | | , Jackie | Son | W | M | Nov | 1888 | | S | | | | Missouri | Missouri | Missouri |
| 30 | | 237 | 239 | | Medlin, S | Head | W | M | Oct | 1858 | 2 | M | 10 | | | Missouri | Tennessee | Missouri |
| 31 | | 238 | 240 | | Estill, Walter D | Head | W | M | Aug | 1874 | 25 | M | 1 | | | Missouri | Kentucky | Missouri |
| 32 | | | | | , Nannie | Wife | W | F | Apr | 1877 | 23 | M | 1 | 1 | 1 | Missouri | Missouri | Missouri |
| 33 | | | | | , Ray | Son | W | M | June | 1899 | 3/12 | S | | | | Missouri | Missouri | Missouri |

America Sartain Family
12th US Census - 1900 - Chariton Township - Howard County, Missouri

## 1910 United States Federal Census for Novle K Willmot

New Mexico › Guadalupe › Cuervo › District 0095

| Street | House No | Visited No | Family No | Name | Relation | Sex | Race | Age | Marital Status | Years Married | Children | Children | Birthplace | Father's | Mother's |
|---|---|---|---|---|---|---|---|---|---|---|---|---|---|---|---|
| | | ✓ | ✓ | , Marvin R | Son | M | W | 10 | S | | | | Illinois | Kentucky | Kentucky |
| | 48 | 48 | | Sartain, America C. | Head | F | W | 65 | Wd | | 9 | 1 | Missouri | Missouri | Kentucky |
| | | | | Willmot, Orville P. | Gran-Son | M | W | 7 | S | | | | Missouri | New York | Missouri |
| | | | | , Novle K. | Gran-Son | M | W | 6 | S | | | | Missouri | New York | Missouri |
| | | | | , William H. | Gran-Son | M | W | 4 | S | | | | Missouri | New York | Missouri |
| | 49 | 49 | | Todd, Clarence E. | Head | M | W | 28 | M | 2 | | | Missouri | Missouri | Missouri |
| | | ✓ | ✓ | , Grace D. | Wife | F | W | 23 | M | 2 | 1 | 0 | Missouri | Missouri | Missouri |
| | 50 | 50 | | Byrd, O. Henry | Head | M | W | 48 | M | 22 | | | Iowa | Illinois | Illinois |

13th US Census - 1910 - America P. Sartain, Orvile P., 'Novle' K., and William H. 'Willmot',
Guadalupe, New Mexico - Cuervo Precinct No. 6

## 1920 United States Federal Census for James A Willmont

Missouri › Lafayette › Middleton › District 0120

| House No. | Dwelling No. | Visited No. | Name | Relation | Home Own | Mortgage | Sex | Race | Age | Marital St | Year Imm | Naturaliz | Year Natu | Attended | Can Read | Can Write | Birthplace |
|---|---|---|---|---|---|---|---|---|---|---|---|---|---|---|---|---|---|
| X | 93 | 99 | Willmont, James A. | head | 1 | R | M | W | 46 | M | | | | | yes | yes | New York |
| | | | Orville | son | | | M | W | 17 | S | | | | yes | yes | yes | Missouri |
| | | | Noble | son | | | M | W | 16 | S | | | | yes | yes | yes | Missouri |
| | | | William | son | | | M | W | 13 | S | | | | yes | yes | yes | Missouri |
| X | 93 | 100 | Champ, Thomas | head | 1 | R | M | W | 45 | M | | | | | yes | yes | Missouri |
| | | | Annie | wife | | | F | W | 31 | M | | | | | yes | yes | Arkansas |
| | | | Dennis | son | | | M | W | 9 | S | | | | yes | | | Oklahoma |
| | | | Mildred | daughter | | | F | W | 7 | S | | | | yes | | | Oklahoma |

James A. 'Willmont' and Sons
14th US Census - 1920 - Middleton Township, Lafayette, Missouri - 2nd Ward of Waverly Town

## 1930 United States Federal Census for William H Wilmot

Missouri › Saline › Arrow Rock › District 0001

| Line No. | Street | Hous No. | Dwelling No. | Family No. | Name | Relation | Home Ow | Home Value | Radio | Farm | Sex | Race | Age | Marital St | Marriage | Attended | Reads & W | Birthplace | Father Birthplace | Mother Birthplace |
|---|---|---|---|---|---|---|---|---|---|---|---|---|---|---|---|---|---|---|---|
| 41 | | | | | Herbert L. | Grandson | | | | | M | W | 15 | S | | yes | | Missouri | Missouri | Missouri |
| 42 | | | 60 | 66 | Biggs, Maybelle B. | Head-w | R | $50 | R | No | F | W | 47 | Wd | 21 | No | yes | Missouri | Missouri | Missouri |
| 43 | | | | | Wilmot, William H. | Boarder | | | | | M | W | 23 | S | | No | yes | Missouri | Missouri | Missouri |
| 44 | | | 61 | 67 | Bradshaw, George W. | Head | O | $1100 | | | M | W | 70 | M | 27 | No | yes | Kentucky | Kentucky | Kentucky |
| 45 | | | | | Sarah A. | Wife-H | | | | | F | W | 65 | M | 18 | No | yes | Missouri | Indiana | Missouri |
| 46 | | | 62 | 68 | Hubbard, William R. | Head | O | $2000 | R | No | M | W | 58 | M | 33 | No | yes | Missouri | Missouri | Missouri |
| 47 | | | | | F. Pearl | Wife-H | | | | | F | W | 46 | M | 21 | No | yes | Missouri | Canada-English | Missouri |
| 48 | | | 63 | 69 | Bradshaw, Benjamin C. | Head | O | $700 | No | | M | W | 68 | M | 35 | No | yes | Kentucky | Kentucky | Kentucky |
| 49 | | | | | E. Virginia | Wife-H | | | | | F | W | 60 | M | 25 | No | yes | Missouri | Missouri | Missouri |
| 50 | | | 64 | 70 | Grimes, Edward P. | Head | O | $1200 | R | No | M | W | 71 | M | 44 | No | yes | Kentucky | Kentucky | Kentucky |

15th US Census - 1930 - William H. Wilmot,
Arrow Rock Township, Saline County, Missouri

### 1930 United States Federal Census for James A Willmot
Missouri › Lafayette › Middleton › District 0028

| Line No. | Street | House No. | Dwelling No. | Family No. | Name | Relation | Home Owned | Home Value | Radio | Farm | Sex | Race | Age | Marital Status | Marriage | Attended | Reads & Writes | Birthplace | Father Birthplace | Mother Birthplace |
|---|---|---|---|---|---|---|---|---|---|---|---|---|---|---|---|---|---|---|---|---|
| 58 | | | | | *[illegible]* | *[illegible]* | | | | | X | W | 37 | S | | | yes | Indiana | Indiana | Indiana |
| 59 | | | | | Elmer | Son | | | | | X | M | 29 | S | | | yes | Missouri | Missouri | Indiana |
| 60 | | | 84 | 84 | Willmot James A | Head | O | | | 70 | M | W | 56 | M | 20 | | yes | Virginia | Virginia | New York |
| 60 | | | | | Bettie | Wife | | | | | X | F | 55 | M | 18 | | yes | Indiana | Indiana | Indiana |
| 61 | | | 85 | 85 | Moore Geo | Head | O | | | | M | W | 40 | S | | | yes | Missouri | Missouri | Missouri |

James A. 'Willmot' - 15th US Census - 1930 -, Middleton Township, Lafayette, Missouri

### 1940 United States Federal Census for James L Wilmat
Missouri › Lafayette › Waverly › 54-31

| Line No. | Street | House No. | Visite No. | Home Owned | Home Value | Farm | Name | Relation | Code A | Sex | Race | Age | Marital Status | Atten School | Grade | Code B | Birthplace |
|---|---|---|---|---|---|---|---|---|---|---|---|---|---|---|---|---|---|
| 35 | | | | | | 1 | erica W | wife | 1 | | W | | | | | | Missouri |
| 36 | | 13 R | | | 12 yes | 1 | Simpson Geo. O | Head | | M | W | 31 | M | 10 | 7 | 7 | Missouri |
| 37 | | | | | | 1 | Grace | wife | 1 | F | W | 24 | M | 10 | 43 | 2 | Missouri |
| 38 | | 14 R | | | 4 yes | | Wilmat James L | Head | c | M | W | 72 | Wd | 10 | 0 | | New York |
| 39 | | | | | | 1 | Carey Luther | Lodger | c | M | W | 75 | Wd | 10 | 0 | | Missouri |
| 40 | | | | | | 1 | Carey W. M. | Lodger | b | M | W | 40 | S | 10 | 6 | 6 | Alabama |

James Wilmot - 16th US Census - 1940
Waverly, Middleton Township, Lafayette County, Missouri

| Line No. | Stree | House No. | Visite No. | Hom Own | Home Value | Farm | Name | Relation | Code A | Sex | Race | Age | Marital Status | Atten Schoo | Grad B | Code | Birthplace |
|---|---|---|---|---|---|---|---|---|---|---|---|---|---|---|---|---|---|
| 20 | | 15.0 | 71 | R | 22 | no | Wilmot, Noble K. | head | | M | C | 36 | m | no | +4 | | Missouri |
| 21 | | | | | | | —, Louise | wife | | F | W | 35 | m | no | H | | Missouri |
| 22 | | | | | | | — Mary Lou | daughter | | F | W | 7 | S | yes | 1 | | Missouri |
| 23 | | 45.0 | 72 | O | 4500 | no | Farkham, Arthur M. | head | | M | W | 43 | m | no | C1 | | Minnesota |
| 24 | | | | | | | — Stella B. | wife | | F | W | 42 | m | no | C1 | | Nebraska |
| 25 | | 4522 | 172 | O | 5500 | no | Hinzie, Charles W. | head | | M | W | 56 | m | no | H4 | | Nebraska |
| 26 | | | | | | | —, Ethel E. | wife | | F | W | 53 | m | no | C2 | | Indiana |
| 27 | | 4524 | 175 | O | 6000 | no | DiGiovrail, Angelo J. | head | | M | W | 35 | m | no | H4 | | Nebraska |

16th US Census - 1940 - Noble K., Louise, and Mary Lou (Lu)
Omaha, Douglas County, Nebraska

# Index

## A

Acadie, Nova Scotia/New
Brunswick
    11, 17
Aghada, County Cork, Ireland
    3-4, 9-11
Aghada Parish/District, County
Cork, Ireland
    9
Ainsworth, W. D.
    46, 126
Anderson, Almira
    50, 63
Arrow Rock, Missouri
    104-105, 107-108

## B

Beau Knot News
    80, 81, 87,
Becknell, William
    107
Bialystoker Synagogue (*see* Willett
    Street Methodist Episcopal
    Church)
Bithele, Mary
    14
Boone, Daniel
    47
Boons Lick, Township, Missouri
    47-48, 132
Boone's Lick Road
    107
Boonesboro, Missouri
    45, 47
Boonesboro Christian Church
Cemetery
    47
Boonville, Missouri
    110
Boston
    14, 17-18
Boyce, William D.
    89
Boy Scouts
    71, 87-89

Brace, Charles Loring
    45, 46
Broome Street, Manhattan, NYC
    22–24, 28, 29, 32, 33, 37, 38

## C

Calvary Cemetery, Woodside, New
York
    14, 24-29, 32, 35, 37, 38, 40, 41,
    119
Canal Street, Manhattan, New York
    20, 35
Carman (*see*: Cartman)
Carson, George W. (Washington)
    45-47, 108
Carson, Christopher Houston 'Kit'
    47, 108
Carson, Lindsey/Rebecca
    47
Cartman
    15, 23, 24, 26, 28, 32
Chariton Township, Howard County
    49, 132
Christie, Bill
    93
Churchtown, County Cork, Ireland
    (*see* Cloyne Parish/District)
Children's Aid Society
    43, 45, 46, 126
Citizens' Military Training Camp
    69-75
Clay County, Missouri
    77, 78
Cline, Charles
    (*see* Kline, Charles)
Cloyne, County Cork, Ireland
    3-5, 7-9, 11, 29
Cloyne Parish/District, County
Cork, Ireland
    7-9
Cognard, 'Cooney'
    90
Cohocton, Steuben, New york
    37
Collan, John and Eleanor (Mullin)
    5, 11
Collan, Mary
    1, 3, 5, 11, 13-15, 17-18, 21,
    24, 28, 33, 35, 127-129, 131

Collins, Mike
    4-5
Coon, Earl H., M.D.
    70
Coppinger, Reverend Dr.
    7
Cork, Ireland
    12, 13, 14
Corps of Engineers
    75, 76, 81, 93
Crabtree
    1, 3, 77, 78, 80, 95, 96
Crabtree, Anna Marie (Foley)
    78
Crabtree, James Allen
    78
Cuervo, Guadalupe County, New
Mexico
    51, 63-64, 101, 102
*Cuervo Clipper* (Newspaper)
    51, 52
Curtis, Roy Emerson
    109, 123

## D

Delancey Street, Manhattan, New
York
    24, 26, 27, 33, 35, 37
DeMolay
    94
Dickens, Charles
    19, 20
DNA
    2, 3,
Duff, John
    58

## E

Ellison Hotel, Santa Rosa, New
Mexico
    51

138

www.ingramcontent.com/pod-product-compliance
Lightning Source LLC
Chambersburg PA
CBHW051617030426
42334CB00030B/3229

*9780578745787*